Walking in Faith: Finding Peace, Strength, and Purpose On Your Journey

By Kay Mulcahy

© 2025 Rapid Response Press, Inc. All rights reserved.

No part of this book may be reproduced, stored in a retrieval system, or transmitted in any form or by any means—electronic, mechanical, photocopying, recording, or otherwise—without the prior written permission of the author, except for brief quotations in reviews or articles.

This book is intended for personal inspiration and growth. The author and publisher make no representations or warranties regarding the completeness or accuracy of the content and assume no liability for any outcomes resulting from its application.

Portions of this book were developed with the assistance of technological tools to aid in research, organization, and drafting. The final manuscript has been thoroughly reviewed, edited, and refined by the author to ensure originality, accuracy, and personal insight.

For permissions requests, inquiries, or additional information, please contact:
Kay Mulcahy
messagesfromtheroad1@gmail.com

ISBN: 978-0-9907674-9-7

FORWARD

Life is a journey filled with moments of joy, seasons of uncertainty, and challenges that test our faith. We often find ourselves searching for peace in the chaos, strength in the struggles, and clarity in the unknown. It is in these moments that we often find ourselves calling out to God and become willing to allow His presence to guide us, His promises to strengthen us, and His love to transform us. When we do this, we find that sense of peace, strength, and clarity we've been seeking. What if we practiced this faith and belief every single day?

This book is a compilation of blog posts I wrote for my website to accompany ***Readings From The Road*** videos I was making on Facebook. As the articles accumulated, I discovered that themes began to emerge that I could categorize, and the idea for a book was born. This book is an invitation to walk in faith—not just in times of certainty, but especially in times of doubt.

It is a call to shift our focus from fear to trust, from worry to worship, and from striving to surrender. Each chapter explores a different aspect of deepening your relationship with God, whether by experiencing His peace, holding onto Him in difficult times, learning to trust His plan, living with love and gratitude, or growing spiritually through transformation.

In **Chapter 1**: Experiencing God's Presence and Peace, we explore how to become more aware of God's love in our daily lives. It is easy to get caught up in the noise of the world, but when we slow down and seek Him, we find a peace that surpasses all understanding.

Chapter 2: Trusting God in Difficult Times reminds us that even in our darkest moments, God never leaves us. When trials arise, we can either let fear take hold or choose to trust that God is working all things for our good. This section provides encouragement and guidance for those struggling to see the light in the midst of challenges.

In **Chapter 3**: Walking in Faith and Trusting God's Plan, we learn how to surrender our own timelines, expectations, and desires to God. His ways are higher than ours, and His timing is always perfect. As we trust Him more fully, we open ourselves up to the miracles and blessings that come with walking in obedience to His will.

Chapter 4: Living a Life of Love, Joy, and Gratitude reminds us that faith is not just about endurance; it is about embracing the fullness of life God has given us. Joy and gratitude are powerful expressions of trust in Him, and through love, we reflect His nature in all we do.

Finally, **Chapter 5**: Spiritual Transformation and Growth guides us toward a deeper understanding of how to live by the Spirit, trust the process, and become more like Christ. The journey of faith is one of continual growth, and when we allow God to work within us, we are transformed into who He created us to be.

This book is not about achieving perfection—it is about learning to walk in faith, even when the path is unclear. As you read through these chapters, may you be encouraged, strengthened, and reminded that you are never alone. God is always with you, guiding you, loving you, and calling you closer to Him. No matter what you face, your victory is already secured in faith.

Let us walk this journey together—one step of faith at a time.

**Walking in Faith: Finding Peace, Strength, and Purpose
On Your Journey**

DEDICATION

I would like to dedicate this book to my loyal followers on Facebook who made this all possible. The love, support, and encouragement from this lovely group inspire me each and every day to strive to know God better and walk the path Jesus would want me to walk.

Walking in Faith: Finding Peace, Strength, and Purpose On Your Journey

CONTENTS

FORWARD III

DEDICATION V

CONTENTS VI

CHAPTER 1 - EXPERIENCING GOD'S PRESENCE AND PEACE 1

How To Feel God's Peaceful Presence 3

God's Love is All Around Us 7

Knowing That God Is Walking Beside You 11

How to Find God in the Chaos and Struggles of Daily Life 15

God's Victory Lives Within You 19

Steps to Recognizing, Nurturing, and Strengthening the Holy Spirit Within You 24

CHAPTER 2 - TRUSTING GOD IN DIFFICULT TIMES 27

Holding Onto God in Trying Times: Trusting That He is Always with You 29

Facing Challenges with Faith: Trusting God in Trying Times 32

Overcoming Troubles with Faith, Not Fear 35

God Goes Before You: Finding Strength and Courage in Him 38

How to Stay Strong in Faith During Trying Times and Trust God to Carry You Through 41

How To Trust God with a Faith That Overcomes 45

CHAPTER 3 - WALKING IN FAITH AND TRUSTING GOD'S PLAN 49

Learning to Walk by Faith, Not Feelings 51

Trusting in God's Perfect Timing: Holding onto Hope While You Wait 55

Walking in God's Will: The Path to Miracles and Blessings 59

Staying Faithful to God: Walking in His Ways Without Seeking the Approval of Others 62

Knowing That God Is Walking Beside You 65

Having Faith in the Plans God Has for You 69

Finding Contentment and Peace Through Life's Ups and Downs .. 74

CHAPTER 4 - LIVING A LIFE OF LOVE, JOY, AND GRATITUDE 79

Living with Joy and Gratitude 81

Understanding God's Perfect Love: A Love That Transforms and Unites 85

How to Live at Peace with Others 89

How To Become More Peaceful by Trusting in God's Promises ... 94

Choosing Peace 97

Your Victory is Secured by Your Faith 101

Shifting Your Focus: From Loss to Blessings 105

CHAPTER 5 - SPIRITUAL TRANSFORMATION AND GROWTH 109

Transforming Yourself by Living in the Spirit of God 111

Developing Self-Belief, Trusting the Process, and Enjoying the Journey 115

Transforming Doubt & Fear into Deeper Faith & Trust 118

Staying Mindful of God in Every Situation & Seeing Life from His Perspective 121

How to Be Like Jesus While on This Earth 126

Learning to Trust God in Times of Distress and Growing in Character 129

AUTHOR'S NOTE 133

ABOUT THE AUTHOR 135

CHAPTER 1 - EXPERIENCING GOD'S PRESENCE AND PEACE

- How To Feel God's Peaceful Presence
- God's Love is All Around Us
- Knowing That God Is Walking Beside You
- How to Find God in the Chaos and Struggles of Daily Life
- God's Victory Lives in You
- Recognizing, Nurturing, and Strengthening the Holy Spirit Within You

Walking in Faith: Finding Peace, Strength, and Purpose
On Your Journey

In a world filled with distractions, stress, and uncertainty, experiencing God's presence and peace can sometimes feel distant. However, the truth is that God is always near, guiding us, loving us, and offering us a peace that surpasses all understanding. This chapter explores how to recognize His presence in our daily lives and embrace the unshakable peace that comes from trusting in Him.

A key part of walking in peace is knowing that God is beside us. When we understand that we are never alone, our fears lose their power, and our faith grows stronger. God walks with us through every joy, trial, and uncertainty, offering guidance, strength, and unwavering support.

In the busyness of life, it is easy to feel disconnected from God, but we can learn how to find Him in the chaos and struggles of daily life. By quieting our minds, seeking Him in prayer, and trusting in His promises, we can become more aware of His presence, even in the most difficult moments.

This chapter serves as a reminder that God's presence is not something we need to search for—it is always with us. As we learn to trust Him more deeply, we will find ourselves enveloped in His peace, walking in His love, and strengthened by the knowledge that He is always by our side.

How To Feel God's Peaceful Presence

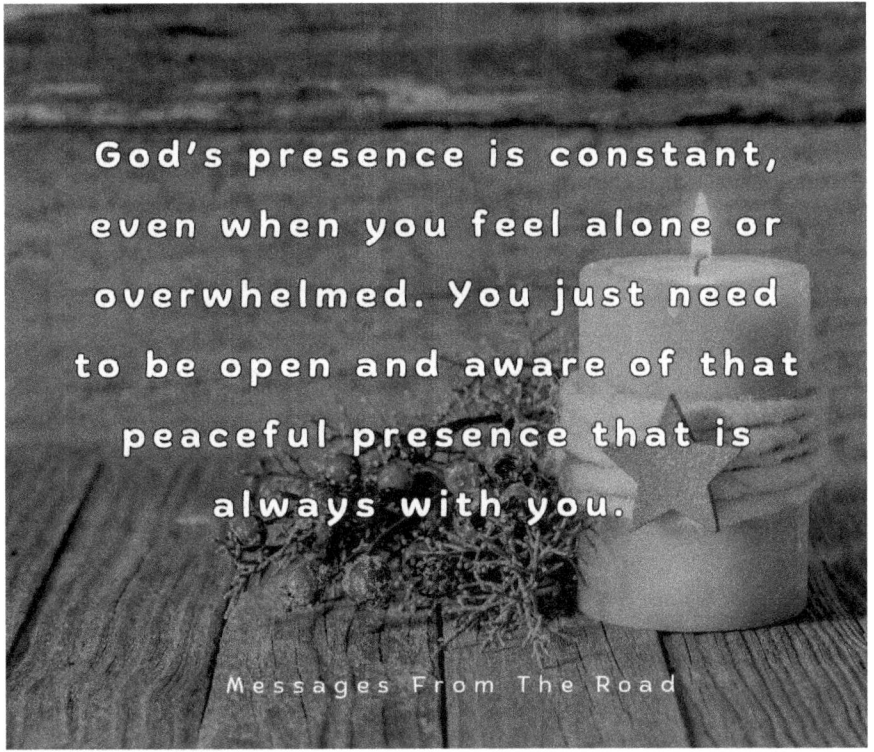

Knowing how close God is to you at all times is a powerful truth that brings comfort, peace, and strength. God's presence is constant, even when you feel alone or overwhelmed. When you intentionally seek Him, you can experience His peace and guidance in profound ways. Here's why this is important and how you can feel His peaceful presence:

The Importance of Knowing God Is Near

- **God's closeness brings comfort in trials:** Knowing He is near reminds you that you are never alone, no matter how difficult life gets.

- **His presence offers peace:** In moments of fear, uncertainty, or stress, His presence calms your spirit and fills you with hope.
- **Closeness to God provides direction:** When you seek Him, He illuminates your path and leads you in His wisdom.

How to Feel God's Peaceful Presence

1. Call on Him in Truth

- Approach God with honesty, sharing your thoughts, fears, and desires. He delights in a sincere heart.
- **Scripture:** *"The Lord is near to all who call on him, to all who call on him in truth."* (**Psalm 145:18**)

2. Spend Time in Prayer

- Prayer is a direct way to communicate with God. It's in these moments of connection that you feel His presence most deeply.
- **Scripture:** *"The Lord is near. Do not be anxious about anything, but in every situation, by prayer and petition, with thanksgiving, present your requests to God."* (**Philippians 4:5-6**)

3. Meditate on His Word

- The Bible is God's voice to you. Reading and reflecting on Scripture invites His truth and peace into your heart.
- **Scripture:** *"Your word is a lamp to my feet and a light to my path."* (**Psalm 119:105**)

4. Worship Him

- Praise and worship shift your focus from problems to God's greatness, drawing you into His presence.

- **Scripture:** *"Come near to God, and he will come near to you."* (**James 4:8**)

5. Practice Stillness

- In the busyness of life, taking time to be still allows you to sense God's nearness.
- **Scripture:** *"Be still, and know that I am God."* (**Psalm 46:10**)

6. Give Thanks in All Circumstances

- Gratitude opens your heart to experience God's peace, even in challenges.
- **Scripture:** *"Give thanks to the Lord, for he is good; his love endures forever."* (**1 Chronicles 16:34**)

7. Rely on the Holy Spirit

- The Holy Spirit is God's presence within you, guiding, comforting, and empowering you. Invite Him into every part of your life.
- **Scripture:** *"And I will ask the Father, and he will give you another advocate to help you and be with you forever—the Spirit of truth."* (**John 14:16-17**)

Living in the Awareness of His Presence

- Begin your day with prayer, asking God to walk with you.
- Carry a verse or a prayer in your heart throughout the day.
- Pause during busy moments to acknowledge His presence.
- End your day by reflecting on how you experienced His closeness.

Final Thought:

By intentionally seeking God and relying on His promises, you can live in constant awareness of His nearness, experiencing His peace and presence in every moment of life.

God's Love is All Around Us

In a world that often feels chaotic and uncertain, there is one constant that never changes—**God's love**. His love is not fleeting or dependent on circumstances; it is unshakable, everlasting, and all-encompassing. Whether we are walking through seasons of joy or moments of deep struggle, His love surrounds us, offering **hope, peace, security, and joy**.

Sometimes, we get so caught up in life's challenges that we fail to recognize the love that is always present. Yet, God reminds us through His Word that He is near, His love is unfailing, and He will never leave us. *"I have loved you with an everlasting love; I have drawn you with unfailing kindness."* (**Jeremiah 31:3**)

Recognizing God's Presence All Around Us

God's presence is all around us, woven into the beauty of everyday moments. He speaks through creation, whispers through small signs, and touches our hearts in ways that remind us we are never alone.

When we take time to slow down and pay attention, we can recognize His gentle presence in countless ways. Keep your eyes and heart open—God is speaking to you every day.

A Glorious Sunset or Sunrise

The breathtaking colors painting the sky remind us of God's artistry and His promise of new beginnings. *"The heavens declare the glory of God; the skies proclaim the work of his hands."* (**Psalm 19:1**)

A Butterfly or Cardinal Crossing Your Path

Butterflies symbolize transformation and renewal, reminding us that God is always working in our lives, bringing beauty from struggle.

A Touching Song at Just the Right Time

Music has a way of speaking to our souls. Whether it's a worship song or a melody that brings peace, God can use music to comfort and encourage us.

Finding a Feather or a Dime

Many believe these small signs serve as gentle reminders that God is watching over us, that angels are near, or that a loved one's love endures beyond this life.

A Gentle Breeze on a Difficult Day

Sometimes, a simple, unexpected breeze can feel like a divine embrace, reminding us that His Spirit is always moving within and around us.

Laughter with Loved Ones

Joy is a gift from God, and moments of laughter and connection with family and friends remind us of His goodness. *"A cheerful heart is good medicine."* **(Proverbs 17:22)**

An Encouraging Word from Someone When You Need It Most

A kind word, a timely message, or even a stranger's smile can be God's way of showing you He sees you and cares for you.

The Stillness of a Quiet Moment

Whether in prayer, reflection, or simply sitting in peace, the stillness reminds us of God's nearness. *"Be still, and know that I am God."* **(Psalm 46:10)**

Ways to Tune Into and Embrace God's Love

To fully embrace this truth, we must open our hearts and intentionally seek His presence. Recognizing God's love in our daily lives allows us to walk with **confidence and peace**, knowing we are never alone. Here are some ways to become more aware of and embrace His deep, abiding love:

1. Spend Time in His Word

The Bible is filled with reminders of God's love. Meditate on scriptures such as **Romans 8:38-39**, which declares that *nothing can separate us from His love.*

2. Look for His Love in Creation

From the beauty of a sunrise to the vastness of the stars, God's love is displayed in everything He has made. Take time to slow down and notice and appreciate His handiwork in the beauty all around you.

3. Seek Him in Prayer

When we draw near to God in prayer, we experience His love in a personal way. **Philippians 4:6-7** reminds us that *through prayer, His peace will guard our hearts and minds.*

4. Recognize His Love Through Others

Acts of kindness, words of encouragement, and the support of loved ones are reflections of God's love. Be open to receiving and sharing that love with those around you.

5. Trust in His Promises

When doubt or fear creeps in, hold onto His promises. **Isaiah 41:10** assures us, *"Do not fear, for I am with you; do not be dismayed, for I am your God. I will strengthen you and help you."*

Final Thought:

God's love is not just something to understand—it is something to **experience and embrace**. When we truly grasp how deeply we are loved, our hearts overflow with **hope, peace, and unshakable joy**.

No matter where you are today, rest in this truth: **You are loved beyond measure, and His love will sustain you through every season of life.**

Knowing That God Is Walking Beside You

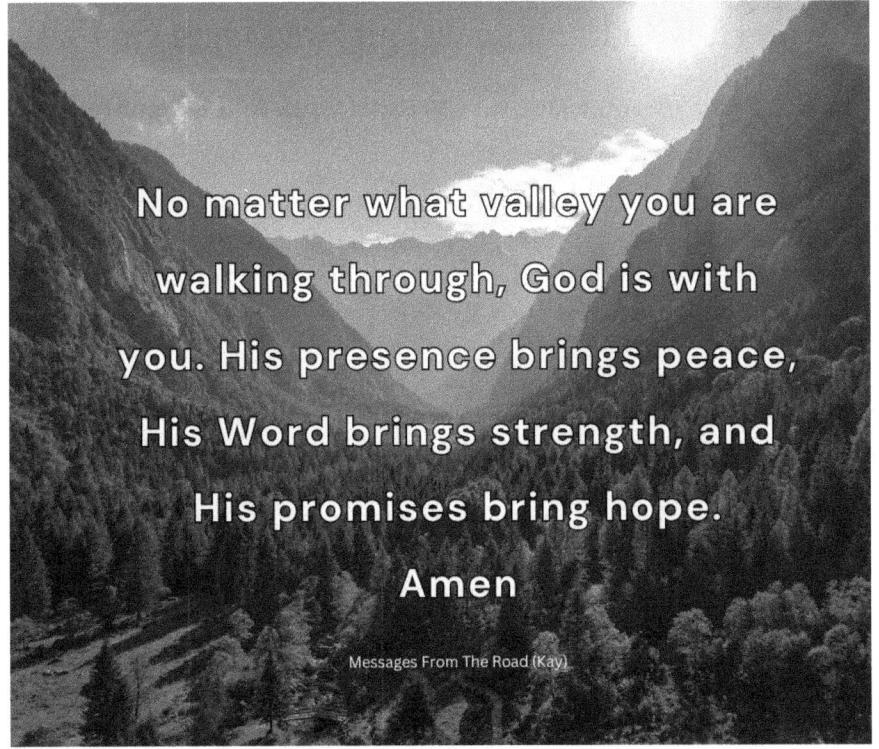

Life is filled with valleys—moments of uncertainty, hardship, and fear. Yet, as believers, we are never alone in these dark places. **Psalm 23:4** offers a powerful reminder of God's presence and protection in our most difficult times:

"Even though I walk through the darkest valley, I will fear no evil, for You are with me; Your rod and Your staff, they comfort me." **(Psalm 23:4, NIV)**

This verse reassures us that no matter how deep or dark our struggles may seem, **God is walking beside us**. His presence brings **peace**, His guidance offers **direction**, and His promises provide **hope**.

Fear does not have to control us when we trust in **the One who holds our future**. But how can we fully embrace the peace that God offers, especially when challenges arise?

How to Experience and Hold Onto God's Peace

Here are some key ways to **experience and hold onto His peace**:

1. Trust in God's Presence

The greatest comfort in **Psalm 23:4** is knowing that **God is with us**. His presence is not distant or conditional—He is always near, even when we cannot feel Him.

Isaiah 41:10 reminds us: *"So do not fear, for I am with you; do not be dismayed, for I am your God. I will strengthen you and help you; I will uphold you with my righteous right hand."*

When fear or doubt creeps in, remind yourself that **God has not abandoned you**. Whisper His name, pray, and **lean into His presence**.

2. Find Strength in His Word

God's promises in Scripture are our foundation of **hope and peace**. When life feels overwhelming, meditate on His words and let them calm your heart.

- *"You will keep in perfect peace those whose minds are steadfast, because they trust in You."* **(Isaiah 26:3)**
- *"The Lord is my light and my salvation—whom shall I fear?"*- **(Psalm 27:1)**

Reading and declaring these verses over your life can **shift your focus from fear to faith**, filling your heart with confidence in God's promises.

3. Pray and Surrender Your Worries to God

Prayer is a powerful way to **release burdens and receive peace**. Instead of holding onto anxiety, lay it at God's feet and trust that He will handle it.

Philippians 4:6-7 encourages us: *"Do not be anxious about anything, but in every situation, by prayer and petition, with thanksgiving, present your requests to God. And the peace of God, which transcends all understanding, will guard your hearts and your minds in Christ Jesus."*

When you feel overwhelmed, take a deep breath and **talk to God**. Surrender your fears, and let His peace guard your heart.

4. Remember That Valleys Are Temporary

Psalm 23:4 says, *"Even though I walk through the darkest valley..."*—not that we remain there forever. Valleys are part of the journey, but **they are not the destination. God is leading you through it**, and He has a purpose for your trials.

- *"Weeping may stay for the night, but rejoicing comes in the morning."* (**Psalm 30:5**)
- *"And we know that in all things God works for the good of those who love Him."* (**Romans 8:28**)

Hold onto the truth that **this season will pass**, and God's goodness will shine through.

5. Lean on God's Guidance and Protection

The "rod and staff" in **Psalm 23:4** symbolize **God's guidance and protection**. Just as a shepherd protects and directs his sheep, **God leads us through life's challenges**, ensuring we are not harmed.

When you feel lost, seek **His direction** through prayer and His Word. **Trust in His perfect guidance** and allow Him to lead you with His wisdom.

Final Thought:

No matter what valley you are walking through, **God is with you**. His presence brings **peace**, His Word brings **strength**, and His promises bring **hope**. When fear tries to take over, stand firm in faith, knowing that **God's light shines even in the darkest places. You are never alone, and His peace is yours to embrace.**

"The Lord is my shepherd; I lack nothing." (Psalm 23:1)

How to Find God in the Chaos and Struggles of Daily Life

> No matter how chaotic life feels, God is always near. He is not distant or silent; He is right beside you, offering strength, peace, and guidance. The key is to invite Him into your daily struggles.
>
> Messages From The Road (Kay)
>
> "God is our refuge and strength, an ever-present help in trouble."
> Psalm 46:1

Life can often feel overwhelming. Between endless responsibilities, unexpected challenges, and the noise of the world around us, it can be hard to feel God's presence. When stress, uncertainty, or struggles take over, we may wonder, "Where is God in all of this?"

But the truth is, **God is always near—working, guiding, and walking with us, even when we don't see or feel Him.**

Psalm 46:1 reminds us, *"God is our refuge and strength, an ever-present help in trouble."* He is not just with us in moments of peace, but right there in the middle of the chaos.

Rather than looking for God only in the big, miraculous moments, we can learn to see Him in **the small, everyday details of our lives.** He speaks through His Word, comforts us in prayer, and reveals His presence in the kindness of others, in nature, and in quiet moments of reflection.

The key is not to wait until life is perfect to seek Him, but to **invite Him into every struggle, every decision, and every ordinary moment.** Below are steps to help you find God even in the busiest, most difficult times and deepen your relationship with Him.

Steps to Finding God in the Chaos and Struggles of Life

1. Start Your Day with God, Even in Small Ways

Before the noise of the world takes over, **set aside time for God, even if it's just a few moments.** Read a short scripture, say a simple prayer, or express gratitude.

Matthew 6:33 reminds us, *"But seek first His kingdom and His righteousness, and all these things will be given to you as well."*

When we prioritize God, everything else begins to fall into place.

2. Turn Your Worries into Prayers

Instead of letting stress consume you, **use it as a reminder to pray.** When anxiety rises, pause and say, *"Lord, I give this to You."*

Philippians 4:6-7 says, *"Do not be anxious about anything, but in every situation, by prayer and petition, with thanksgiving, present your requests to God. And the peace of God, which transcends all understanding, will guard your hearts and your minds in Christ Jesus."*

Prayer shifts our focus from fear to faith.

3. Find God in the Small, Everyday Moments

God is not just in church services or dramatic miracles—He is in **the sunrise, a child's laughter, the kindness of a stranger, and the quiet moments of peace.**

Psalm 19:1 says, *"The heavens declare the glory of God; the skies proclaim the work of His hands."*

Train your heart to recognize His presence in the simple things.

4. Read and Meditate on God's Word

When life is chaotic, **scripture is a source of clarity and strength.** Even if you read just one verse a day, let God's Word guide and encourage you.

Psalm 119:105 says, *"Your word is a lamp for my feet, a light on my path."*

His Word reminds us that we are never alone, no matter how difficult things may seem.

5. Stay Connected with Other Believers

Whether through church, Bible study, or faith-filled friendships, **God often speaks through the support and wisdom of others.**

Hebrews 10:24-25 says, *"And let us consider how we may spur one another on toward love and good deeds, not giving up meeting together, as some are in the habit of doing, but encouraging one another."*

Surround yourself with people who encourage your faith.

6. Trust God's Plan, Even When You Don't Understand

Life's struggles can make us feel lost, but **God sees the bigger picture.** Trust that He is working things out for your good, even when the path isn't clear.

Romans 8:28 reminds us, *"And we know that in all things God works for the good of those who love Him, who have been called according to His purpose."*

Even in pain, God is shaping something beautiful.

7. Rest in God's Presence, Even in the Chaos

Sometimes, **we just need to pause and be still before God.** When the world feels heavy, take a deep breath and sit in His presence.

Exodus 14:14 says, *"The Lord will fight for you; you need only to be still."*

In stillness, we find His peace and strength.

Final Thought:

No matter how chaotic life feels, **God is always near.** He is not distant or silent; He is right beside you, offering strength, peace, and guidance.

The key is to **invite Him into your daily struggles**—to talk to Him, listen for His voice, and trust His plan.

Isaiah 41:10 reminds us, *"So do not fear, for I am with you; do not be dismayed, for I am your God. I will strengthen you and help you; I will uphold you with my righteous right hand."*

You don't have to wait for perfect circumstances to find God—He is here, in this moment, walking with you through every joy and every challenge. **Keep seeking Him, and you will find that He has been with you all along.**

God's Victory Lives Within You

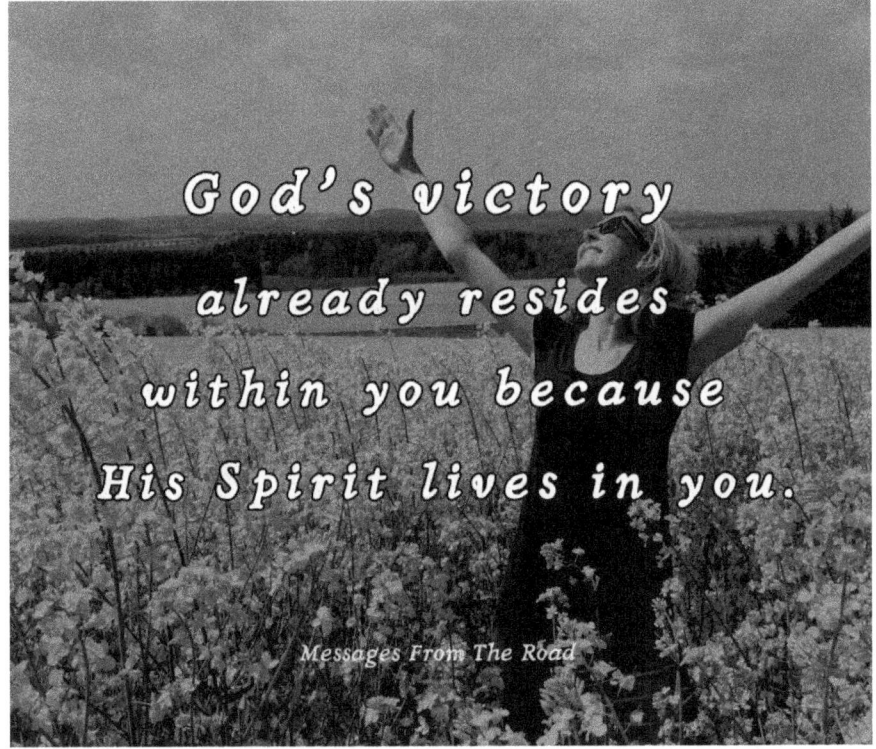

How to Live Victoriously as God Wants for You

Do you realize that the victory God has called you to walk already lives within you? To fully recognize and capitalize on this requires faith, surrender, and a shift in perspective.

The idea that God has equipped us with everything we need to live victoriously is a big thing to grasp, but all we need to do is learn to quiet our hearts, listen to His voice, and step into that truth. Here's how:

1. Acknowledge the Victory That Already Lives Within You

The moment we place our faith in Jesus, His Spirit dwells within us, empowering us to walk in victory. This is not a future promise but a present reality.

As **1 John 4:4** reminds us: *"You, dear children, are from God and have overcome them because the one who is in you is greater than the one who is in the world."*

Victory isn't about striving but about trusting the power of God already at work within us.

2. Still Your Heart Before God

In the rush of life, it's easy to feel overwhelmed and disconnected from God's truth. To hear His guidance and embrace His victory, we must quiet the noise and enter His presence.

Psalm 46:10 says: *"Be still, and know that I am God."*

Stillness allows us to align our hearts with His, hear His whispers, and walk the path He's showing us. Set aside intentional time to pray, reflect, and meditate on His Word.

3. Declare and Stand on God's Promises

Victory begins with recognizing and believing God's promises for your life. His Word is filled with declarations of His power, provision, and victory.

For example: *"But thanks be to God! He gives us the victory through our Lord Jesus Christ."* — **1 Corinthians 15:57**

Declare these promises daily, not just as words but as truths you fully embrace. Faith turns promises into realities.

4. Walk by Faith, Not by Sight

Living in victory doesn't always mean we see immediate results or avoid challenges. Instead, it's about trusting God's plan even when the path seems unclear.

As **2 Corinthians 5:7** encourages: *"For we walk by faith, not by sight."*

Faith reminds us that God's victory is often unfolding behind the scenes, and our job is to keep moving forward in obedience.

5. Surrender Your Battles to God

Victory doesn't come from our strength but from surrendering to God and letting Him fight on our behalf.

Exodus 14:14 promises: *"The Lord will fight for you; you need only to be still."*

When we release control and trust Him fully, we step into His victory and experience His peace.

6. Live Out Your Identity in Christ

You are more than a conqueror through Christ.

Romans 8:37 declares *"No, in all these things we are more than conquerors through him who loved us".*

Recognizing your identity as a beloved child of God, equipped and empowered, transforms how you approach life's challenges. You are not striving for victory—you're living from it.

7. Take Spirit-Led Action

Victory isn't passive; it's a walk of faith. As you still your heart before God, He will show you the path forward:

"Whether you turn to the right or to the left, your ears will hear a voice behind you, saying, 'This is the way; walk in it.'" — **Isaiah 30:21**

Obey His promptings, step out boldly, and trust that He is guiding your steps.

8. Celebrate the Victories, Big and Small

Every step forward is a sign of God's victory in your life. Celebrate progress, no matter how small, as a reminder of God's faithfulness.

"Rejoice always, pray continually, give thanks in all circumstances; for this is God's will for you in Christ Jesus." — **1 Thessalonians 5:16**

Gratitude fuels faith and helps you recognize His work in your life.

Final Thought:

God's victory already resides within you because His Spirit lives in you. As you quiet your heart before Him, embrace His promises, and walk in obedience, you'll see that His path leads to peace, strength, and victory. Trust that He has already won the battles ahead of you, and rest in the confidence that His power is working through you.

"The Lord your God is with you, the Mighty Warrior who saves. He will take great delight in you; in His love He will no longer rebuke you but will rejoice over you with singing." — **Zephaniah 3:17**

The Holy Spirit is God's gift to us—a divine presence that guides, strengthens, and empowers us in our daily lives. Jesus promised in **John 14:16-17 (NIV)**, *"And I will ask the Father, and He will give you another advocate to help you and be with you forever—the Spirit of truth."*

When we welcome the Holy Spirit into our hearts, we gain access to a peace that transcends understanding, a strength that carries us through challenges, and a confidence that comes from knowing we are never alone.

Yet, many of us struggle to recognize the presence of the Spirit or feel disconnected from His power. How do we truly experience the Spirit's flow in our lives? How can we nurture this divine presence and allow it to transform us? In the following steps, we will explore practical and spiritual ways to cultivate the Holy Spirit within us so that we can walk boldly in faith and purpose.

Steps to Recognizing, Nurturing, and Strengthening the Holy Spirit Within You

The journey of faith is not meant to be walked in our own strength. God has given us the gift of the Holy Spirit—our Helper, Comforter, and Guide. By learning to recognize His presence, nurture His work within us, and strengthen our walk with Him, we open the door to deeper peace, wisdom, and courage in our daily lives.

Steps to Recognizing, Nurturing, and Strengthening the Holy Spirit Within You

1. Create Space for the Holy Spirit Through Prayer and Stillness

The Holy Spirit speaks in moments of stillness, but we often drown out His voice with the noise of the world. Set aside time each day for quiet prayer and reflection.

Invite the Spirit to guide you, just as David prayed in **Psalm 143:10 (NIV),** *"Teach me to do Your will, for You are my God; may Your good Spirit lead me on level ground."*

Action: Begin each day with a simple prayer: *"Holy Spirit, fill me today. Lead me, teach me, and strengthen me in all I do."*

2. Immerse Yourself in God's Word

The Spirit moves through Scripture, revealing truth and wisdom. When we meditate on God's Word, we strengthen our spiritual connection.

Jesus said in John 6:63 (NIV), *"The Spirit gives life; the flesh counts for nothing. The words I have spoken to you—they are full of the Spirit and life."*

Action: Read a passage of Scripture daily, asking the Holy Spirit to reveal its meaning for your life. Keep a journal to reflect on insights.

3. Walk in Obedience and Surrender

The more we yield to the Spirit's leading, the stronger His presence becomes in our lives. When we obey God's direction, we align ourselves with His will and experience His power.

Galatians 5:25 (NIV) reminds us, *"Since we live by the Spirit, let us keep in step with the Spirit."*

Action: Pay attention to nudges from the Holy Spirit—whether to encourage someone, step out in faith, or let go of something holding you back. Act in obedience and trust God's guidance.

4. Surround Yourself with Faith-Filled Community

God never intended for us to walk alone. The Spirit works through the body of Christ, strengthening and encouraging us.

Proverbs 27:17 (NIV) says, *"As iron sharpens iron, so one person sharpens another."*

Action: Join a Bible study, church group, or faith-based community where you can grow spiritually and be encouraged in your walk.

5. Step Out in Faith with Boldness

The Holy Spirit fills us with confidence and courage to fulfill God's purpose for our lives. When we trust Him fully, fear loses its grip.

2 Timothy 1:7 (NIV) declares, *"For the Spirit God gave us does not make us timid, but gives us power, love, and self-discipline."*

Action: Ask God for the courage to step out in faith—whether it's sharing your testimony, serving in ministry, or embracing a new challenge.

Final Thought:

When we recognize, nurture, and surrender to the Holy Spirit, we walk in divine confidence and strength. The more we seek Him, the more He fills us with His presence, transforming our hearts and minds.

Romans 15:13 (NIV) offers a beautiful blessing: *"May the God of hope fill you with all joy and peace as you trust in Him, so that you may overflow with hope by the power of the Holy Spirit."*

Let this be your daily prayer—to be filled, led, and strengthened by the Holy Spirit. As you walk in His presence, may you find unshakable confidence, peace beyond understanding, and the courage to live out your faith boldly.

CHAPTER 2 - TRUSTING GOD IN DIFFICULT TIMES

- Holding Onto God in Trying Times: Trusting That He is Always with You
- Facing Challenges with Faith: Trusting God in Trying Times
- Overcoming Troubles with Faith, Not Fear
- God Goes Before You: Finding Strength and Courage in Him
- How to Stay Strong in Faith During Trying Times and Trust God to Carry You Through
- How To Trust God with a Faith That Overcomes

Walking in Faith: Finding Peace, Strength, and Purpose On Your Journey

Life is filled with challenges, uncertainties, and moments that test our faith. In these trying times, we often struggle with fear, doubt, and the temptation to rely on our own strength.

However, God calls us to trust in Him, knowing that He is always with us, guiding us, and working all things for our good. This chapter explores how to hold onto faith during difficulties, lean on God's promises, and find strength in His presence.

Fear often stands in the way of faith, which is why it is crucial to **overcome troubles with faith, not fear.** Fear paralyzes us, but faith moves us forward. By leaning on God's Word and trusting His promises, we can silence fear and walk confidently in His plan.

A powerful truth that sustains us during hard times is that **God goes before us.** He is not only with us but also ahead of us, preparing the way, strengthening us, and ensuring that we are never alone in our struggles. His presence gives us the courage to move forward, even when the path is uncertain.

This chapter reminds us that no trial is greater than God's power, and no storm is beyond His control. When we trust in Him, we find the strength, courage, and faith to navigate life's hardest moments with confidence. No matter what we face, God is with us—guiding us, fighting for us, and carrying us through.

Holding Onto God in Trying Times: Trusting That He is Always with You

Life is filled with seasons of joy and peace, but it also brings challenges that test our faith. There are moments when **pain, uncertainty, or loss make us question where God is or why we are facing such difficulties.**

It can be tempting to feel abandoned or discouraged, wondering if our prayers are being heard. But the truth is, **God never leaves us.** Even in our darkest moments, He is working behind the scenes, strengthening us and drawing us closer to Him.

Faith is not about always feeling strong—it's about choosing to trust God even when everything around us seems uncertain. **Hebrews 11:1** reminds us, *"Now faith is confidence in what we hope for and assurance about what we do not see."*

How to Hold Onto God in Difficult Times

Holding onto God during hard times requires us to **lean on His promises, seek Him in prayer, and trust that He is guiding us even when we don't understand.** Below are steps to help you remain firm in your faith and experience God's presence, even in the midst of trials.

1. Lean on God's Promises in Scripture

God's Word is a source of **strength, hope, and truth.** When trials come, remind yourself of His promises.

Isaiah 41:10 says, *"So do not fear, for I am with you; do not be dismayed, for I am your God. I will strengthen you and help you; I will uphold you with my righteous right hand."*

Meditate on scripture daily, allowing His truth to renew your mind and strengthen your faith.

2. Pray Without Ceasing

Prayer is our direct line to God. When life feels overwhelming, **bring your worries, fears, and doubts to Him.** He hears you, and He cares.

Philippians 4:6-7 encourages us, *"Do not be anxious about anything, but in every situation, by prayer and petition, with thanksgiving, present your requests to God. And the peace of God, which transcends all understanding, will guard your hearts and your minds in Christ Jesus."*

Even when you don't have the words, simply call out to Him, and He will meet you where you are.

3. Trust That God is Working, Even When You Can't See It

God's plans are often beyond our understanding. We may not see the full picture, but we can trust that He is at work.

Romans 8:28 assures us, *"And we know that in all things God works for the good of those who love Him, who have been called according to His purpose."*

Even in pain, He is shaping something beautiful.

4. Surround Yourself with Faithful Community

We are not meant to go through hardships alone. **Stay connected with fellow believers who can encourage you, pray with you, and remind you of God's truth.**

Hebrews 10:24-25 says, *"And let us consider how we may spur one another on toward love and good deeds, not giving up meeting together, as some are in the habit of doing, but encouraging one another."*

Fellowship strengthens our faith and helps us keep our focus on God.

5. Worship and Praise Through the Storm

Worship shifts our perspective from problems to **God's greatness.** Even in difficulty, praising God brings peace and strengthens our trust in Him.

Psalm 34:1 says, *"I will bless the Lord at all times; His praise shall continually be in my mouth."*

No matter the situation, worship reminds us that **God is bigger than our struggles.**

6. Let Go and Surrender to God's Plan

Holding onto fear and control only weighs us down. Instead, choose to **surrender your worries and trust in God's perfect plan.**

Proverbs 3:5-6 says, *"Trust in the Lord with all your heart and lean not on your own understanding; in all your ways submit to Him, and He will make your paths straight."*

Even when things don't go as expected, surrendering allows us to walk in **peace, knowing He is leading the way.**

Final Thought:

No matter what trials you are facing, **you are never alone.** God is not distant—He is **walking with you, strengthening you, and holding you in His love.** Even when life feels heavy, His presence remains steadfast.

Deuteronomy 31:8 reassures us, *"The Lord Himself goes before you and will be with you; He will never leave you nor forsake you. Do not be afraid; do not be discouraged."*

Hold onto God's promises, seek Him daily, and trust that He is carrying you through. **The storm will pass, but His love and faithfulness will never fail.**

Keep believing, keep praying, and keep your eyes fixed on Him—**for He is your refuge, your strength, and your ever-present help in times of trouble.**

Facing Challenges with Faith: Trusting God in Trying Times

Life is filled with challenges, uncertainties, and moments that test our strength and resilience. In these trying times, it is easy to feel overwhelmed, discouraged, and even question our purpose. But as believers, we have a firm foundation: **God is with us**.

He does not allow difficulties in our lives to destroy us but to refine us, teach us, and increase our faith. Every obstacle is an opportunity for growth, a stepping stone toward a stronger relationship with Him. Instead of fearing trials, we can embrace them with confidence, knowing that God is using them for our good (**Romans 8:28**).

Seeing Obstacles as Opportunities

When we encounter difficulties, our natural response may be frustration or fear. However, God calls us to view them from a different perspective.

James 1:2-4 reminds us, *"Consider it pure joy, my brothers and sisters, whenever you face trials of many kinds, because you know that the testing of your faith produces perseverance. Let perseverance finish its work so that you may be mature and complete, not lacking anything."*

Trials are not setbacks; they are setups for greater faith and deeper trust in God. Here are a few ways to shift our mindset and view obstacles as opportunities:

1. Seek God's Purpose in the Struggle

Instead of asking, "Why is this happening to me?" ask, "What is God trying to teach me?" Every challenge carries a lesson designed to shape our character and draw us closer to God (**Romans 5:3-5**).

2. Trust in God's Strength, Not Your Own

When we feel weak, God's power is made perfect in us (**2 Corinthians 12:9-10**). Our struggles remind us that we are not meant to carry our burdens alone; God is our ever-present help in times of trouble (**Psalm 46:1**).

3. Pray with Expectation

In difficult times, our prayers should not just be pleas for relief but also declarations of faith. **Philippians 4:6-7** tells us to present our requests to God with thanksgiving, and His peace will guard our hearts and minds.

4. Take Action in Faith

Faith is not passive; it requires us to move forward even when we do not see the full picture. **Hebrews 11:1** defines faith as *"confidence in what we hope for and assurance about what we do not see."* Trusting God means stepping out even when the path ahead is unclear.

Putting God's Promises to the Proof

God has given us His promises, and He is always faithful to fulfill them. When we face challenges, we must stand firm on His Word and put His promises into action:

- **God will provide for your needs:** *"And my God will meet all your needs according to the riches of His glory in Christ Jesus."* (**Philippians 4:19**) When financial struggles arise, trust that God is your provider.

- **God will give you peace:** *"You will keep in perfect peace those whose minds are steadfast because they trust in you."* (**Isaiah 26:3**) When anxiety creeps in, lean into His peace.

- **God will strengthen you:** *"But those who hope in the Lord will renew their strength; they will soar on wings like eagles."* (**Isaiah 40:31**) When you feel weak, draw on His strength.

- **God will never leave you:** *"Never will I leave you; never will I forsake you."* (**Hebrews 13:5**) When loneliness strikes, remember that God is always by your side.

Final Thought:

Difficulties are a part of life, but they do not define us—our faith does. Instead of letting trials shake our trust in God, we can allow them to deepen our faith, refine our character, and draw us closer to Him. Every challenge is an invitation to experience God's power and faithfulness in new ways.

When tested, stand firm, knowing that He is using your struggles for His glory and your ultimate good. So, walk boldly in faith, face every obstacle with confidence, and trust that with God by your side, you are never alone and never defeated.

Overcoming Troubles with Faith, Not Fear

Life is full of challenges, and it is natural to feel fear when faced with uncertainty, hardship, or pain. However, God calls us to trust Him completely, knowing that He is always with us. When we look at our troubles through His eyes, we see not defeat, but victory; not despair, but hope.

Isaiah 41:10 reminds us, *"Fear not, for I am with you; be not dismayed, for I am your God; I will strengthen you, I will help you, I will uphold you with my righteous right hand."*

Instead of reacting to trials with fear, we must learn to stand in faith, believing in God's promises and trusting that He will never leave or forsake us.

Steps for Overcoming Your Troubles With Faith

Here are key steps to help you walk in faith and overcome your troubles with confidence in God.

1. Acknowledge God's Presence in Every Situation

When troubles arise, the first step is to remind yourself that **you are not alone.** God is with you in every situation, working things out for your good.

Deuteronomy 31:6 assures us, *"Be strong and courageous. Do not fear or be in dread of them, for it is the Lord your God who goes with you. He will not leave you or forsake you."*

Instead of focusing on the size of your problems, focus on the greatness of your God.

2. Shift Your Perspective—See Through God's Eyes

We often view trials as obstacles, but through God's eyes, they are opportunities for growth and breakthrough.

Romans 8:28 reminds us, *"And we know that in all things God works for the good of those who love Him, who have been called according to His purpose."* Instead of asking, *"Why is this happening to me?"* ask, *"What is God teaching me through this?"*

Trust that He is shaping you for something greater.

3. Stand on God's Promises

God's Word is filled with promises of protection, provision, and peace. Meditate on Scriptures that remind you of His faithfulness.

Joshua 1:9 declares, *"Have I not commanded you? Be strong and courageous. Do not be afraid; do not be discouraged, for the Lord your God will be with you wherever you go."*

Speak His promises over your life and declare victory, even before you see it.

4. Cast Your Worries on God and Pray Without Ceasing

Fear grows when we dwell on our problems, but faith grows when we give them to God.

1 Peter 5:7 says, *"Cast all your anxieties on Him, because He cares for you."* Instead of holding onto fear, release your worries in prayer.

Philippians 4:6-7 instructs us, *"Do not be anxious about anything, but in every situation, by prayer and petition, with thanksgiving, present your requests to God. And the peace of God, which transcends all understanding, will guard your hearts and your minds in Christ Jesus."*

When worries arise, pause and turn them into a prayer, releasing them to God with thanksgiving.

5. Walk by Faith, Not by Sight

It's easy to trust God when things are going well, but true faith is believing even when we can't see the outcome.

2 Corinthians 5:7 reminds us, *"For we walk by faith, not by sight."*

Even when circumstances seem hopeless, believe that God is in control and that He will bring you through stronger than before.

6. Surround Yourself with Encouragement

Faith flourishes in the right environment. Stay connected to God's Word, worship, and people who encourage your faith.

Hebrews 10:23-25 urges us, *"Let us hold unswervingly to the hope we profess, for He who promised is faithful... encouraging one another—and all the more as you see the Day approaching."*

When you surround yourself with truth and encouragement, fear loses its grip on you.

7. Praise God Even in the Storm

Worship shifts our focus from our problems to the greatness of God. When Paul and Silas were imprisoned, they prayed and sang hymns to God, and their chains were broken.

But at midnight Paul and Silas were praying and singing hymns to God, and the other prisoners were listening to them. 26 Suddenly there was such a violent earthquake that the foundations of the prison were shaken. At once all the prison doors flew open, and everyone's chains came loose. (**Acts 16:25-26**).

Instead of letting troubles bring you down, praise God in the midst of them, knowing that He is already working on your behalf.

Final Thought:

Fear may try to rise, but it does not have to control you. When you choose faith over fear, trust over doubt, and praise over worry, you align yourself with God's power and promises.

Isaiah 43:2 assures us, *"When you pass through the waters, I will be with you; and when you pass through the rivers, they will not sweep over you. When you walk through the fire, you will not be burned; the flames will not set you ablaze."*

No matter what you face, **God is with you, guiding you, strengthening you, and leading you to victory.** Trust Him, see your troubles through His eyes, and walk forward with confidence, knowing that

His promises never fail.

God Goes Before You: Finding Strength and Courage in Him

Life is full of challenges that can leave us feeling uncertain, fearful, and overwhelmed. But as followers of Christ, we are never alone—God goes before us, walks beside us, and strengthens us in every battle we face.

Deuteronomy 31:8 assures us, *"The Lord Himself goes before you and will be with you; He will never leave you nor forsake you. Do not be afraid; do not be discouraged."* True courage is not about being fearless on our own but about trusting in God's strength to carry us through.

Bravery is not about relying on human strength or confidence, but in knowing that God is fighting for us. We don't have to muster up courage on our own—**it is God's power working in us that makes us strong.**

Isaiah 41:10 says, *"So do not fear, for I am with you; do not be dismayed, for I am your God. I will strengthen you and help you; I will uphold you with my righteous right hand."* When we lean on Him, we can move forward boldly, knowing that He has already prepared the way.

Steps to Walking in God's Strength and Courage

1. Acknowledge That True Strength Comes from God

We often try to handle things on our own, but true bravery comes from surrendering to God's strength.

Philippians 4:13 says, *"I can do all things through Christ who strengthens me."*

Instead of depending on your own abilities, rely on His power, knowing that He is more than able to equip you for any challenge.

2. Trust That God Goes Before You

God is not only with you—He has already gone ahead of you, preparing the way.

Exodus 13:21 tells us, *"By day the Lord went ahead of them in a pillar of cloud to guide them on their way and by night in a pillar of fire to give them light."*

When you trust that God is already making a way, you can step forward with confidence.

3. Replace Fear with Faith

Fear can paralyze us, but faith empowers us to move forward.

2 Timothy 1:7 reminds us, *"For God gave us a spirit not of fear but of power and love and self-control."*

When fear creeps in, replace it with faith by declaring God's promises over your life.

4. Stand on God's Promises in Difficult Moments

Whenever you feel weak, remind yourself of God's Word.

Joshua 1:9 says, *"Have I not commanded you? Be strong and courageous. Do not be afraid; do not be discouraged, for the Lord your God will be with you wherever you go."*

Meditating on His promises will fill you with confidence to face any situation.

5. Take Bold Steps of Obedience

Courage is not the absence of fear but choosing to trust God despite it. Step out in faith, knowing that God is with you.

Psalm 56:3-4 says, *"When I am afraid, I put my trust in You. In God, whose word I praise—in God I trust and am not afraid."*

Even when the path seems uncertain, obedience to God will always lead to victory.

6. Pray for Strength and Guidance

Ask God daily for the courage to face challenges with boldness.

Psalm 138:3 says, *"On the day I called, You answered me; You made me bold with strength in my soul."*

When you feel weak, turn to Him in prayer, and He will fill you with His power.

7. Surround Yourself with Encouraging Faith

The people around you can either build your faith or feed your fear.

Hebrews 10:24-25 encourages us to *"consider how we may spur one another on toward love and good deeds... encouraging one another."*

Stay connected to those who strengthen your faith and remind you of God's power in your life.

Final Thought:

You don't have to be brave on your own—God is your source of strength. When you feel fear creeping in, remind yourself that **God goes before you, walks beside you, and fights for you.**

Psalm 27:1 declares, *"The Lord is my light and my salvation—whom shall I fear? The Lord is the stronghold of my life—of whom shall I be afraid?"*

With God on your side, you can walk through any challenge with confidence, knowing that **He is your strength, your protector, and your guide.** Let go of fear, step forward in faith, and trust that God is leading you into victory!

Walking in Faith: Finding Peace, Strength, and Purpose On Your Journey

How to Stay Strong in Faith During Trying Times and Trust God to Carry You Through

Life is full of challenges, and God never promised that it would be easy. Instead, He assures us that trials will come, but they are opportunities for growth and a testament to our faith.

Jesus said in **John 16:33**: *"I have told you these things, so that in me you may have peace. In this world you will have trouble. But take heart! I have overcome the world."*

God calls us to trust Him in every season, knowing that He is faithful to see us through. When we endure trials with unwavering faith, we grow closer to Him and receive His eternal promises.

James 1:12 reminds us: *"Blessed is the one who perseveres under trial because, having stood the test, that person will receive the crown of life that the Lord has promised to those who love Him."*

Trusting God to Carry You Through During Trying Times

Here are some practical ways to stay strong in faith during trying times and trust God to carry you through:

1. Hold Firm to God's Promises in Scripture

The Word of God is a source of hope and reassurance. Meditate on verses that remind you of His faithfulness and love.

Isaiah 41:10 says: *"So do not fear, for I am with you; do not be dismayed, for I am your God. I will strengthen you and help you; I will uphold you with my righteous right hand."*

When doubt creeps in, let His promises anchor your soul.

2. Pray Without Ceasing

Prayer is your direct line to God. In trials, pour out your heart to Him and ask for His strength and guidance.

Philippians 4:6-7 encourages us: *"Do not be anxious about anything, but in every situation, by prayer and petition, with thanksgiving, present your requests to God. And the peace of God, which transcends all understanding, will guard your hearts and your minds in Christ Jesus."*

Through prayer, you invite God's peace to calm your spirit.

3. Trust in God's Plan

Even when life feels uncertain, trust that God is working all things for good.

Romans 8:28 reminds us: *"And we know that in all things God works for the good of those who love Him, who have been called according to His purpose."*

Remember, your trials have a purpose, and God's plan is greater than you can imagine.

4. Lean on God's Strength, Not Your Own

It's natural to feel weak during difficult times, but God's power is made perfect in weakness.

As Paul said in **2 Corinthians 12:9**: *"But He said to me, 'My grace is sufficient for you, for My power is made perfect in weakness.' Therefore, I will boast all the more gladly about my weaknesses, so that Christ's power may rest on me."*

Surrender your struggles to Him, and let His strength sustain you.

5. Surround Yourself with Faithful Community

Don't face trials alone. Seek encouragement and support from fellow believers.

Hebrews 10:24-25 says: *"And let us consider how we may spur one another on toward love and good deeds, not giving up meeting together, as some are in the habit of doing, but encouraging one another—and all the more as you see the Day approaching."*

Community reminds you that you are not alone and that others can pray with and for you.

6. Rejoice in Trials as Opportunities for Growth

Trials refine our character and deepen our relationship with God.

James 1:2-4 teaches us: *"Consider it pure joy, my brothers and sisters, whenever you face trials of many kinds, because you know that the testing of your faith produces perseverance. Let perseverance finish its work so that you may be mature and complete, not lacking anything."*

Though difficult, trials shape you into the person God created you to be.

7. Keep an Eternal Perspective

Remember, this life is temporary, and the trials we face are momentary compared to the eternal glory to come.

2 Corinthians 4:17-18 reminds us: *"For our light and momentary troubles are achieving for us an eternal glory that far outweighs them all. So we fix our eyes not on what is seen, but on what is unseen, since what is seen is temporary, but what is unseen is eternal."*

Focus on the eternal reward awaiting you, and let that hope sustain you.

8. Worship and Give Thanks

Worship shifts your focus from your problems to God's greatness. Even in trials, find reasons to thank Him for His goodness.

Psalm 34:1 says: *"I will bless the Lord at all times; His praise will continually be in my mouth."*

When you worship, you declare your trust in God, no matter the circumstances.

Final Thought:

Staying strong in faith during trials requires a deliberate choice to trust God, lean on His promises, and seek His strength daily. As you persevere, remember that God is with you, refining your faith and preparing you for His eternal rewards.

Trust Him, for He is faithful to carry you through every storm.

**Walking in Faith: Finding Peace, Strength, and Purpose
On Your Journey**

> When trials come, we can choose to let them shake our faith or strengthen it.

How To Trust God with a Faith That Overcomes

Life is full of moments that test our faith—times when the weight of uncertainty, pain, or disappointment makes us question if God is truly present. Unanswered prayers, unexpected hardships, and prolonged struggles can create doubt, making it difficult to hold onto trust. However, these obstacles are not meant to destroy our faith; rather, they are opportunities for it to grow.

God understands our struggles with unbelief. Even some of the strongest figures in the Bible wrestled with doubt, yet they learned to trust Him more deeply through their trials.

Mark 9:24 (NIV) captures the cry of a father desperate for his child's healing: *"I do believe; help me overcome my unbelief!"* This heartfelt plea reminds us that faith and doubt can coexist, but through God's grace, our trust in Him can be strengthened.

Steps to Navigating Major Challenges With Unwavering Faith

So how do we overcome unbelief and continue trusting God, even when life is difficult? Let's explore key steps to help us navigate challenges with unwavering faith.

1. Acknowledge Your Doubts and Bring Them to God

One of the most important things to remember is that God is not afraid of our doubts. He invites us to bring them to Him in honesty and prayer. In **Psalm 62:8 (NIV)**, we are reminded, *"Trust in Him at all times, you people; pour out your hearts to Him, for God is our refuge."*

When you struggle to believe, don't hide your feelings—bring them to God in prayer. Ask Him to strengthen your faith, just as the disciples did when they asked, *"Lord, increase our faith!"* (**Luke 17:5, NIV**). Trust begins with a conversation, and God is always listening.

Action Step: Set aside time each day to talk to God honestly about your struggles. Keep a journal of your prayers and reflect on how He answers in ways you may not have expected.

2. Stand on God's Promises, Not Your Feelings

Our emotions are ever-changing, but God's promises remain the same. When unbelief creeps in, we must anchor ourselves in His Word. **Romans 10:17 (NIV)** tells us, *"Faith comes from hearing the message, and the message is heard through the word about Christ."*

By immersing ourselves in Scripture, we replace doubt with truth. When we remind ourselves of God's faithfulness in the past, we gain confidence that He will be faithful in the present and future.

Action Step: Memorize key scriptures that reinforce God's promises. When doubt arises, speak these verses out loud as a declaration of faith. Some powerful verses include:

- **Proverbs 3:5-6 (NIV)**: *"Trust in the Lord with all your heart and lean not on your own understanding."*
- **Isaiah 41:10 (NIV)**: *"Do not fear, for I am with you; do not be dismayed, for I am your God."*

3. Shift Your Perspective: See Obstacles as Opportunities for Faith

Trials are not a sign that God has abandoned us; rather, they are a chance to strengthen our trust in Him. **James 1:2-3 (NIV)** encourages us, *"Consider it pure joy, my brothers and sisters, whenever you face trials of many kinds, because you know that the testing of your faith produces perseverance."*

Every obstacle we face is an invitation to deepen our reliance on God. When we shift our mindset from fear to faith, we begin to see trials not as barriers but as stepping stones to spiritual growth.

Action Step: When you face difficulties, pause and ask yourself, *"How can this situation increase my faith?"* Choose to see challenges as an opportunity for God to show His power in your life.

4. Surround Yourself with Faith-Filled Community

Doubt grows in isolation, but faith is strengthened in community. **Proverbs 27:17 (NIV)** states, *"As iron sharpens iron, so one person sharpens another."* When we surround ourselves with others who encourage and uplift us, we are reminded of God's presence in our lives.

Fellowship with believers provides wisdom, support, and accountability. Their testimonies of how God has worked in their lives can serve as a source of inspiration and encouragement when our faith is wavering.

Action Step: Engage in a faith-based community—whether it's a church group, a Bible study, or a close circle of faith-driven friends. Share your struggles and encourage one another in faith.

5. Take One Step of Faith at a Time

Faith is not about having all the answers; it's about trusting God one step at a time. **Hebrews 11:1 (NIV)** defines faith as *"confidence in what we hope for and assurance about what we do not see."* Even when we don't understand the bigger picture, we can take small, daily steps of trust.

Peter walked on water not because he understood how, but because he focused on Jesus (**Matthew 14:29-31**). When he looked at the waves, fear took over. The same is true for us—when we fix our eyes on our problems, doubt creeps in, but when we focus on God, we find the courage to move forward.

Action Step: Identify one area of your life where you need to trust God more. Take a small step of faith today, even if it feels uncomfortable.

Final Thought:

Overcoming unbelief is not about having perfect faith—it's about continuing to trust, even when we don't have all the answers. When trials come, we can choose to let them shake our faith or strengthen it.

Remember, God is patient with us. He meets us in our doubts, just as He did with Thomas (**John 20:27**), and He strengthens our faith when we seek Him. Trust is a journey, and every obstacle we face is an opportunity to grow closer to Him.

As you walk forward, hold onto this promise from **Isaiah 26:3 (NIV)**: *"You will keep in perfect peace those whose minds are steadfast, because they trust in You."* Keep pressing on, keep believing, and watch as God moves in your life in ways beyond what you could ever imagine.

You are not alone. Keep the faith and let your trust in God grow stronger with every step.

**Walking in Faith: Finding Peace, Strength, and Purpose
On Your Journey**

CHAPTER 3 - WALKING IN FAITH AND TRUSTING GOD'S PLAN

- Learning to Walk by Faith, Not Feelings
- Trusting in God's Perfect Timing: Holding Onto Hope While You Wait
- Walking in God's Will: The Path to Miracles and Blessings
- Staying Faithful to God: Walking in His Ways Without Seeking the Approval of Others
- Knowing That God is Walking Beside You
- Having Faith in the Plans God Has For You
- Finding Contentment and Peace Through Life's Ups and Downs

Walking in Faith: Finding Peace, Strength, and Purpose On Your Journey

Faith is not just believing in God when life is easy—it is trusting Him when the path is unclear, when waiting feels unbearable, and when His plan seems different from our own.

Walking in faith means surrendering our own desires, fears, and expectations, choosing instead to trust that God's timing and purpose are always perfect. This chapter explores how to live by faith, trust God's plan, and experience the blessings that come from walking in obedience to Him.

One of the greatest challenges in faith is trusting in God's perfect timing. It is difficult to wait when we don't see immediate answers, but God's delays are never His denials. He is always working behind the scenes, aligning everything according to His will. When we learn to trust His timing, we find peace in the waiting and assurance in His promises.

In a world that often seeks approval from others, we must remember the importance of staying faithful to God without seeking the validation of people. True faith means standing firm in God's truth, even when it goes against societal norms or expectations. When we seek His approval above all else, we live with a sense of purpose and unwavering confidence.

This chapter is a reminder that faith is a journey, not a destination. It is about trusting God daily, even when we don't have all the answers. As we walk in faith and surrender to His plan, we will experience the fullness of His blessings, the peace of His presence, and the joy of knowing that He is always guiding our steps.

Learning to Walk by Faith, Not Feelings

Life is full of uncertainties, doubts, and fears, but true faith is not about having all the answers—it is about trusting God even in the midst of uncertainty. Our emotions can shift like the wind, but God's presence remains constant.

To build a faith that is unwavering, we must learn to rely not on how we feel in the moment, but on the truth of God's Word and His promises. As **2 Corinthians 5:7** reminds us, *"For we walk by faith, not by sight."*

Steps for Strengthening Your Faith in All Circumstances

This journey is not about eliminating doubt but about pressing forward through it, knowing that God is near, guiding each step. Here are steps to strengthen your faith and trust in Him, even when emotions and circumstances try to shake you.

1. Ground Yourself in God's Word

Feelings can be deceptive, but God's Word is unchanging. When fear and uncertainty rise, turn to Scripture for reassurance.

Isaiah 41:10 declares, *"Fear not, for I am with you; be not dismayed, for I am your God. I will strengthen you, I will help you, I will uphold you with my righteous right hand."*

Make a habit of reading and meditating on His promises daily.

2. Pray Honestly and Consistently

Faith is not about ignoring your feelings, but about surrendering them to God.

In **Philippians 4:6-7**, we are reminded, *"Do not be anxious about anything, but in everything by prayer and supplication with thanksgiving let your requests be made known to God. And the peace of God, which surpasses all understanding, will guard your hearts and your minds in Christ Jesus."*

Talk to God openly about your doubts and fears, and let His peace cover you.

3. Step Forward Despite Uncertainty

Faith is not found in certainty, but in moving forward even when you don't see the whole path.

Like Peter stepping out of the boat in **Matthew 14:29-31**, we must trust Jesus enough to walk even when the waves of life seem overwhelming. Even if we falter, His hand is always there to catch us.

4. Remember Past Victories

When you struggle with doubt, look back on the times God has been faithful in your life.

Psalm 77:11 says, *"I will remember the deeds of the Lord; yes, I will remember your wonders of old."*

Keep a journal of answered prayers and moments of God's faithfulness to remind yourself that He has never left you and never will.

5. Surround Yourself with Faith-Filled Community

Faith grows stronger when we walk alongside other believers.

Hebrews 10:25 encourages us, *"Not neglecting to meet together, as is the habit of some, but encouraging one another."*

Find a church, small group, or friends who will lift you up, speak truth into your life, and pray for you during moments of doubt. Our

Messages From The Road Facebook Community is an excellent example of a group of people who will lift you up and pray for you.

6. Let the Good News Guide Your Steps

The Gospel is not just about salvation—it is about walking in victory every day.

Ephesians 6:15 describes faith as having *"your feet fitted with the readiness that comes from the gospel of peace."*

No matter what challenges come, let the good news of Christ be the foundation that directs your path.

7. Trust That You Will Overcome

God has already declared victory over your life.

Romans 8:37 assures us, *"In all these things we are more than conquerors through Him who loved us."*

No matter what you face, trust that God is leading you to overcome, and let His promises, not your feelings, shape your steps.

By choosing faith over feelings, you will discover that even in doubt and uncertainty, God is always near. Walk forward with confidence, knowing that His love and guidance are steadfast, and He will lead you through every trial into victory.

Final Thought:

Faith is not about never feeling afraid, uncertain, or overwhelmed—it is about trusting God even when those emotions arise. True faith is forged in the fire of doubt, strengthened through uncertainty, and proven in the moments when we choose to walk forward despite not seeing the whole path.

As we root ourselves in Scripture, pray with honesty, step forward in trust, remember God's past faithfulness, surround ourselves with fellow believers, and allow the Gospel to guide our steps, we will find that our faith becomes stronger than our fears.

God's presence is not dependent on how we feel—He is with us always. **Deuteronomy 31:8** reminds us, *"The Lord himself goes before you and will be with you; he will never leave you nor forsake you. Do not be afraid; do not be discouraged."*

So let us move forward with unwavering trust, allowing faith—not feelings—to direct our steps. No matter what challenges come, we can stand firm, knowing that we are more than conquerors through Christ who strengthens us.

Trusting in God's Perfect Timing: Holding onto Hope While You Wait

Waiting is one of the hardest things to do, especially when we are believing God for something—whether it's a breakthrough, an answered prayer, or a long-awaited dream. When things don't happen as quickly as we expect, it's easy to become discouraged, frustrated, or even question if God has forgotten us.

But the truth is, **God's timing is always perfect.** He sees what we cannot, and His plans unfold exactly when they are meant to. **Ecclesiastes 3:11** reminds us, *"He has made everything beautiful in its time."* This means that while we may not always understand the delays, we can trust that **God is preparing us, shaping us, and working behind the scenes** for our ultimate good.

How to Trust in God's Timing and Stay Hopeful While Waiting

Instead of giving up hope, we can learn to wait with faith, patience, and confidence in His divine plan. Here's how:

1. Remember That God's Plans Are Higher Than Ours

It's natural to want things to happen on our schedule, but God operates on a divine timeline.

Isaiah 55:8-9 says, *"For my thoughts are not your thoughts, neither are your ways my ways,"* declares the Lord. *"As the heavens are higher than the earth, so are my ways higher than your ways and my thoughts than your thoughts."*

Trusting His timing means believing that **His wisdom is greater than ours** and that He knows what is best for us.

2. Stay Rooted in God's Promises

When waiting feels difficult, turn to Scripture for encouragement. **God's Word is filled with promises of His faithfulness.**

Habakkuk 2:3 says, *"For the vision is yet for an appointed time; it hastens toward the goal and it will not fail. Though it delays, wait for it; for it will certainly come, it will not delay."*

Cling to His promises and **remind yourself daily that He is trustworthy.**

3. Keep Praying and Seeking God

Waiting is not a time of inactivity—it's a time to draw closer to God. **Instead of focusing on what hasn't happened yet, focus on deepening your relationship with Him.**

Philippians 4:6-7 encourages us, *"Do not be anxious about anything, but in every situation, by prayer and petition, with thanksgiving, present your requests to God. And the peace of God, which transcends all understanding, will guard your hearts and your minds in Christ Jesus."*

Prayer not only brings peace, but it also aligns our hearts with God's will.

4. Be Patient and Trust the Process

Patience is a difficult but necessary part of faith.

James 1:3-4 reminds us, *"Because you know that the testing of your faith produces perseverance. Let perseverance finish its work so that you may be mature and complete, not lacking anything."*

Every season of waiting is an opportunity for **growth, refinement, and preparation.** God is working **in you** just as much as He is working on the situation you are waiting for.

5. Look Back at How God Has Been Faithful Before

Reflect on past times when you waited on God and saw His faithfulness come through. **If He was faithful then, He will be faithful now.**

Lamentations 3:22-23 says, *"Because of the Lord's great love we are not consumed, for His compassions never fail. They are new every morning; great is Your faithfulness."*

Let His past goodness remind you that He is always working in your life.

6. Find Joy in the Present Season

Instead of being consumed by what hasn't happened yet, **focus on the blessings of today.** God wants us to enjoy the present moment while trusting Him for the future.

Psalm 118:24 says, *"This is the day that the Lord has made; let us rejoice and be glad in it."*

There is joy to be found in every season—don't miss it by being too focused on what's next.

7. Let Go of Control and Fully Surrender to God

At the heart of trusting God's timing is surrender. **Let go of the need to control the outcome and trust that His plan is far better than anything we could create for ourselves.**

Proverbs 3:5-6 instructs us, *"Trust in the Lord with all your heart and lean not on your own understanding; in all your ways submit to Him, and He will make your paths straight."*

The moment we fully surrender is the moment we experience **His peace and guidance.**

Final Thought:

Even when it feels like nothing is happening, **God is always moving, always working, and always preparing something greater than we can imagine.** His delays are not denials—they are divine appointments. While you wait, **keep trusting, keep praying, and keep believing** that His plans for you are good.

Jeremiah 29:11 reassures us, *"For I know the plans I have for you," declares the Lord, "plans to prosper you and not to harm you, plans to give you hope and a future."*

Walking in God's Will: The Path to Miracles and Blessings

Living in alignment with God's will is the key to unlocking the fullness of His blessings and miracles in our lives. When we surrender our own plans and seek to do His will more and more, **we begin to walk in the divine purpose He has set for us.** This journey of obedience does not always mean an easy road, but it is a road filled with **peace, provision, and the manifestation of God's promises.**

Jesus Himself taught us the power of doing God's will when He said, *"My food is to do the will of Him who sent me and to finish His work."* (**John 4:34**). When we seek to **follow God's direction rather than our own desires, we step into a life where miracles happen— not just in extraordinary ways, but in our daily walk as we experience His guidance, favor, and transformation.**

How Doing God's Will Opens the Door to Miracles and Blessings

1. Walking in Obedience Brings Divine Favor

When we obey God's word and follow His leading, we position ourselves to receive His divine favor.

Deuteronomy 28:1-2 says, *"If you fully obey the Lord your God and carefully follow all His commands I give you today, the Lord your God will set you high above all the nations on earth. All these blessings will come on you and accompany you if you obey the Lord your God."*

Blessings follow obedience. Even when it feels difficult, trusting God's path over our own leads to **His supernatural provision, protection, and favor** in our lives.

2. Aligning with God's Will Positions Us for Miracles

Many of the great miracles in the Bible happened when people stepped out in **faithful obedience.**

The Red Sea parted when Moses lifted his staff (**Exodus 14:21**), the walls of Jericho fell when Joshua and the Israelites followed God's unconventional battle plan (**Joshua 6:20**), and Peter walked on water when he obeyed Jesus' call (**Matthew 14:29**).

When we say **"yes"** to God—especially when we don't fully understand—**we create space for Him to work miracles in our lives.**

3. Faithfulness Leads to God's Promises Being Fulfilled

God's promises are not just empty words; they are meant to be experienced. However, many of these promises are unlocked through **faithful action.**

Psalm 37:4-5 says, *"Take delight in the Lord, and He will give you the desires of your heart. Commit your way to the Lord; trust in Him and He will do this."*

When we commit to **seeking Him first** in all that we do, we start to see **His blessings unfold in ways beyond what we could have imagined.**

4. Doing God's Will Transforms Our Hearts and Lives

As we consistently walk in obedience, we experience not just **external blessings, but an internal transformation.** We begin to love deeper, have more peace, and live with a greater sense of **purpose and joy.**

Romans 12:2 reminds us, *"Do not conform to the pattern of this world, but be transformed by the renewing of your mind. Then you will be able to test and approve what God's will is—His good, pleasing and perfect will."*

By following His will, **our desires shift to align with His desires, and our lives become a reflection of His grace and love.**

5. Trusting God's Plan Brings Supernatural Peace

One of the greatest miracles we can experience is **unshakable peace, even in the midst of trials.** When we are in alignment with God's will, we don't have to **strive, stress, or fear the future—because we know He is in control.**

Philippians 4:6-7 tells us, *"Do not be anxious about anything, but in every situation, by prayer and petition, with thanksgiving, present your requests to God. And the peace of God, which transcends all understanding, will guard your hearts and your minds in Christ Jesus."*

Living in His will allows us to **release worry and rest in the assurance of His divine plan.**

Final Thought:

The more we surrender to God and align our lives with His will, **the more we experience the power of His promises.** Blessings, miracles, and divine provision follow those who **walk by faith and trust in Him completely.**

Even when we don't see immediate results, we can be confident that **God is working behind the scenes for our good. Jeremiah 29:11** reassures us, *"For I know the plans I have for you,"* declares the Lord, *"plans to prosper you and not to harm you, plans to give you hope and a future."*

Staying Faithful to God: Walking in His Ways Without Seeking the Approval of Others

In a world that constantly pressures us to conform, staying faithful to God requires strength, commitment, and an unwavering trust in His plan. It can be tempting to seek the approval of others, but as believers, our true purpose is to live in alignment with **God's will**, not the world's expectations.

Galatians 1:10 reminds us, *"Am I now trying to win the approval of human beings, or of God? Or am I trying to please people? If I were still trying to please people, I would not be a servant of Christ."*

Staying Faithful to God Without Needing Others' Approval

Here are some practical ways to stay faithful to God and walk in His ways, free from the need for human validation:

1. Seek God's Approval Above All Else

The only approval that truly matters is God's. When you focus on **pleasing Him**, you find purpose and fulfillment that no human approval can provide.

Colossians 3:23 says, *"Whatever you do, work at it with all your heart, as working for the Lord, not for human masters."*

2. Stay Rooted in His Word

The Bible is our guide for living a life that honors God. Reading and meditating on His Word daily helps us discern His ways from the world's distractions.

Psalm 119:105 reminds us, *"Your word is a lamp to my feet and a light for my path."*

3. Strengthen Your Relationship with God Through Prayer

Talking to God regularly keeps your heart aligned with His. When you pray, seek His wisdom, ask for His strength, and trust in His guidance rather than looking to people for validation.

Philippians 4:6-7 encourages us to *bring everything to God in prayer and experience His peace.*

4. Surround Yourself with Godly Influences

The people you spend time with can either strengthen or weaken your faith. Choose to walk with those who encourage your spiritual growth and hold you accountable in love.

Proverbs 27:17 says, *"As iron sharpens iron, so one person sharpens another."*

5. Live by Faith, Not by Fear of Rejection

Choosing to walk in God's ways may lead to rejection by the world, but Jesus Himself faced the same.

He reminds us in **John 15:18**, *"If the world hates you, keep in mind that it hated me first."* Stay strong in your faith, knowing that God's favor is far greater than the world's approval.

6. Obey God, Even When It's Hard

Faithfulness to God requires obedience, even when it goes against popular opinion.

Joshua 1:9 encourages us, *"Be strong and courageous. Do not be afraid; do not be discouraged, for the Lord your God will be with you wherever you go."* Trust that His ways lead to the best outcome.

7. Remember Your Identity in Christ

You are **a child of God**, deeply loved and chosen by Him. Your worth is not determined by what others think, but by who God says you are.

1 Peter 2:9 declares, *"But you are a chosen people, a royal priesthood, a holy nation, God's special possession, that you may declare the praises of Him who called you out of darkness into His wonderful light."*

Final Thought:

Staying faithful to God and walking in His ways means trusting that **His plan is greater than any human opinion**. When you choose to follow Him wholeheartedly, you will find **peace, purpose, and fulfillment** that no worldly approval can provide. Keep your eyes on Him, and He will direct your path (Proverbs 3:5-6).

Walk boldly in faith, knowing that God is always with you!

Walking in Faith: Finding Peace, Strength, and Purpose On Your Journey

Knowing That God Is Walking Beside You

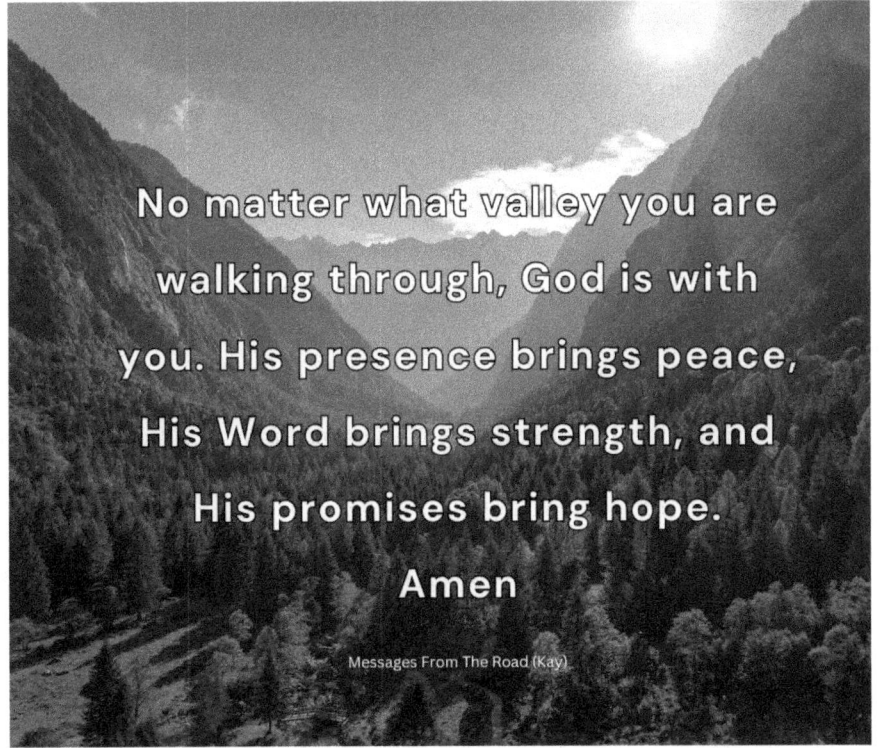

Life is filled with valleys—moments of uncertainty, hardship, and fear. Yet, as believers, we are never alone in these dark places. **Psalm 23:4** offers a powerful reminder of God's presence and protection in our most difficult times:

"Even though I walk through the darkest valley, I will fear no evil, for You are with me; Your rod and Your staff, they comfort me." **(Psalm 23:4, NIV)**

This verse reassures us that no matter how deep or dark our struggles may seem, **God is walking beside us**. His presence brings **peace**, His guidance offers **direction**, and His promises provide **hope**.

Fear does not have to control us when we trust in **the One who holds our future**.

How to Embrace God's Peace in the Midst of Challenges

But how can we fully embrace the peace that God offers, especially when challenges arise? Here are some key ways to **experience and hold onto His peace**:

1. Trust in God's Presence

The greatest comfort in **Psalm 23:4** is knowing that **God is with us**. His presence is not distant or conditional—He is always near, even when we cannot feel Him.

Isaiah 41:10 reminds us: *"So do not fear, for I am with you; do not be dismayed, for I am your God. I will strengthen you and help you; I will uphold you with my righteous right hand."*

When fear or doubt creeps in, remind yourself that **God has not abandoned you**. Whisper His name, pray, and **lean into His presence**.

2. Find Strength in His Word

God's promises in Scripture are our foundation of **hope and peace**. When life feels overwhelming, meditate on His words and let them calm your heart.

- *"You will keep in perfect peace those whose minds are steadfast, because they trust in You."* (Isaiah 26:3)
- *"The Lord is my light and my salvation—whom shall I fear?"* (Psalm 27:1)

Reading and declaring these verses over your life can **shift your focus from fear to faith**, filling your heart with confidence in God's promises.

3. Pray and Surrender Your Worries to God

Prayer is a powerful way to **release burdens and receive peace**. Instead of holding onto anxiety, lay it at God's feet and trust that He will handle it.

Philippians 4:6-7 encourages us: *"Do not be anxious about anything, but in every situation, by prayer and petition, with thanksgiving, present your requests to God. And the peace of God, which transcends all understanding, will guard your hearts and your minds in Christ Jesus."*

When you feel overwhelmed, take a deep breath and **talk to God**. Surrender your fears, and let His peace guard your heart.

4. Remember That Valleys Are Temporary

Psalm 23:4 says, *"Even though I walk through the darkest valley..."*—not that we remain there forever. Valleys are part of the journey, but **they are not the destination. God is leading you through it**, and He has a purpose for your trials.

- *"Weeping may stay for the night, but rejoicing comes in the morning."* (**Psalm 30:5**)
- *"And we know that in all things God works for the good of those who love Him."* (**Romans 8:28**)

Hold onto the truth that **this season will pass**, and God's goodness will shine through.

5. Lean on God's Guidance and Protection

The "rod and staff" in **Psalm 23:4** symbolize **God's guidance and protection**. Just as a shepherd protects and directs his sheep, **God leads us through life's challenges**, ensuring we are not harmed.

When you feel lost, seek **His direction** through prayer and His Word. **Trust in His perfect guidance** and allow Him to lead you with His wisdom.

Final Thought: God is with you.

No matter what valley you are walking through, **God is with you**. His presence brings **peace**, His Word brings **strength**, and His promises bring **hope**. When fear tries to take over, stand firm in faith, knowing that **God's light shines even in the darkest places. You are never alone, and His peace is yours to embrace.**

"The Lord is my shepherd; I lack nothing." (Psalm 23:1)

Walking in Faith: Finding Peace, Strength, and Purpose
On Your Journey

Having Faith in the Plans God Has for You

Having faith in God that His plans for you are inconceivably amazing is about trusting His infinite wisdom, love, and sovereignty even when life feels uncertain or challenging. It's believing that God, who created you with purpose and knows you intimately, has plans for your life that are far beyond what you could imagine.

Trusting that God Has a Plan for You

Are you struggling to believe that God has a plan for you? Here are some steps you can take to build and hold onto faith that God not only has a plan for you, but that it is better than anything you could conceive of on your own:

1. Trusting in God's Goodness and Love

- God's plans for you are rooted in His love and desire for your ultimate good. He sees the bigger picture, including the blessings, growth, and opportunities that lie ahead.
- *"For I know the plans I have for you," declares the Lord, "plans to prosper you and not to harm you, plans to give you hope and a future"* (**Jeremiah 29:11**).
- **Faith in Action:**
    - Remind yourself daily that God is for you, not against you.
    - Meditate on His promises and trust that His love never fails.

2. Believing in God's Sovereignty

- Even when life feels chaotic or unpredictable, God is in control. His plans are not hindered by circumstances or human limitations.

- *"Many are the plans in a person's heart, but it is the Lord's purpose that prevails"* (**Proverbs 19:21**).
- **Faith in Action:**
    - Release your worries to God, knowing He is guiding every step.
    - Trust that delays, detours, or disappointments are part of His greater purpose.

3. Embracing the Mystery of His Plans

- God's ways are higher than ours, and His plans often surpass our understanding. What may seem unclear or difficult now will eventually make sense in His perfect timing.
- *"As the heavens are higher than the earth, so are my ways higher than your ways and my thoughts than your thoughts"* (**Isaiah 55:9**).
- **Faith in Action:**
    - Be patient when you don't see immediate results.
    - Acknowledge that God's vision for your life is greater than your own.

4. Walking by Faith, Not by Sight

- Faith requires trusting God even when you cannot see how everything will unfold. It's a daily decision to follow His lead, believing that His plans are unfolding for your good.
- *"Now faith is confidence in what we hope for and assurance about what we do not see"* (**Hebrews 11:1**).
- **Faith in Action:**
    - Take steps of faith, even if you feel uncertain.
    - Trust that God will provide clarity and resources as you move forward.

5. Finding Peace in His Timing

- God's plans are not only perfect in design but also in timing. He knows when you're ready for the blessings He has prepared for you.
- *"He has made everything beautiful in its time"* (**Ecclesiastes 3:11**).
- **Faith in Action:**
    - Let go of impatience or the urge to control outcomes.
    - Trust that God's timing is always better than your own.

6. Celebrating the Promise of Abundant Life

- God's plans for you include an abundant life—not necessarily free from challenges but filled with His presence, purpose, and peace.
- *"I have come that they may have life, and have it to the full"* (**John 10:10**).
- **Faith in Action:**
    - Focus on the blessings already in your life as evidence of His faithfulness.
    - Anticipate the amazing things He will do in the future.

7. Strengthening Faith Through Prayer and Scripture

- Prayer keeps you connected to God's heart, while Scripture reminds you of His promises and faithfulness. Together, they build your faith in His plans.
- *"Commit to the Lord whatever you do, and He will establish your plans"* (**Proverbs 16:3**).
- **Faith in Action:**
    - Spend time daily in prayer, asking God to align your desires with His plans.
    - Study the Bible to deepen your understanding of His promises.

8. Trusting That Your Pain Has Purpose

- God can use your challenges and pain to refine you and prepare you for the incredible plans He has for you.
- *"And we know that in all things God works for the good of those who love Him, who have been called according to His purpose"* (**Romans 8:28**).
- **Faith in Action:**
    - View trials as opportunities for growth and trust that God is working behind the scenes.
    - Lean on His strength when you feel weak or discouraged.

9. Celebrating God's Faithfulness

- Reflect on the ways God has worked in your life before. This will remind you of His ability to fulfill His promises.
- *"I will remember the deeds of the Lord; yes, I will remember your miracles of long ago"* (**Psalm 77:11**).
- **Faith in Action:**
    - Keep a journal of answered prayers and blessings as a testimony of God's faithfulness.
    - Share your story with others to encourage them to trust in God's plans.

10. Living with Expectation

- Trusting that God's plans are inconceivably amazing fills your life with hope and expectation. Each day becomes an opportunity to see His hand at work.
- *"No eye has seen, no ear has heard, and no mind has imagined what God has prepared for those who love Him"* (**1 Corinthians 2:9**).
- **Faith in Action:**
    - Wake up each day expecting God to move in your life.
    - Keep your heart and mind open to His leading and blessings.

Final Thought:

When you trust that God's plans for you are beyond anything you could imagine, you can live with hope, joy, and peace, knowing that your future is secure in His hands. With faith as your foundation, you can confidently face each day, assured that God's purpose for your life is unfolding in ways more amazing than you could ever conceive.

Finding Contentment and Peace Through Life's Ups and Downs

Life is a journey filled with highs and lows, moments of joy and seasons of struggle. It's easy to feel content when everything is going well, but when challenges arise, uncertainty and anxiety can steal our peace. However, true contentment doesn't come from perfect circumstances—it comes from within, rooted in faith and trust in God's plan.

The Apostle Paul understood this well when he wrote in **Philippians 4:11-12 (NIV):** *"I have learned to be content whatever the circumstances. I know what it is to be in need, and I know what it is to have plenty. I have learned the secret of being content in any and every situation."*

Daily Practice for Cultivating Inner Peace

So how do we cultivate this kind of peace and contentment, regardless of what life throws our way? It takes daily practice and a heart anchored in God. Here are some steps to help you embrace contentment no matter what season you're in.

1. Shift Your Focus from Circumstances to God

Contentment begins when we stop looking to external things—money, success, relationships—to bring us lasting happiness. These things may bring temporary joy, but they are not the foundation of true peace. Instead, we find contentment by fixing our eyes on God.

Isaiah 26:3 (NIV) reminds us: *"You will keep in perfect peace those whose minds are steadfast, because they trust in you."*

Daily Practice: Begin each morning by focusing on God rather than your circumstances. Read Scripture, pray, and remind yourself that no matter what happens today, He is in control.

2. Practice Gratitude in All Situations

Gratitude is one of the most powerful ways to cultivate contentment. When we focus on what we have rather than what we lack, our perspective shifts. Even in difficult times, there is always something to be thankful for.

1 Thessalonians 5:16-18 (NIV) encourages us: *"Rejoice always, pray continually, give thanks in all circumstances; for this is God's will for you in Christ Jesus."*

Daily Practice: Keep a gratitude journal. Each day, write down three things you're thankful for, no matter how big or small. This habit will train your heart to see the blessings in every situation.

3. Let Go of Comparison

Comparison is a thief of joy. In a world filled with social media and constant reminders of what others have, it's easy to feel like we're missing out. But contentment comes when we stop comparing our lives to others and focus on our unique journey with God.

Galatians 6:4 (NIV) says: *"Each one should test their own actions. Then they can take pride in themselves alone, without comparing themselves to someone else."*

Daily Practice: When you find yourself comparing, pause and shift your focus. Remind yourself of God's specific blessings in your life and His unique plan for you.

4. Trust God's Timing and Plan

Much of our discontent comes from wanting things to happen on our timeline. We get frustrated when prayers seem unanswered or when life isn't unfolding the way we expected. But true peace comes from trusting that God's plan is perfect, even when we don't understand it.

Proverbs 3:5-6 (NIV) assures us: *"Trust in the Lord with all your heart and lean not on your own understanding; in all your ways submit to him, and he will make your paths straight."*

Daily Practice: When you feel impatient or discouraged, take a deep breath and surrender your plans to God. Pray for peace and trust that He is working things out for your good.

5. Live in the Present Moment

Worrying about the past or future robs us of peace. Contentment grows when we learn to be fully present in today, embracing the moment without fear of what's ahead. Jesus Himself reminded us not to be anxious about tomorrow.

Matthew 6:34 (NIV) says: *"Therefore do not worry about tomorrow, for tomorrow will worry about itself. Each day has enough trouble of its own."*

Daily Practice: When your mind drifts to worry, bring yourself back to the present. Take a deep breath, focus on the blessings of today, and trust that God has tomorrow in His hands.

Final Thought:

Contentment is not about having a perfect life—it's about having a heart that trusts God in every season. When we shift our focus from circumstances to God, practice gratitude, let go of comparison, trust His timing, and live in the present, we open our hearts to a peace that surpasses all understanding.

Philippians 4:6-7 (NIV) reminds us: *"Do not be anxious about anything, but in every situation, by prayer and petition, with thanksgiving, present your requests to God. And the peace of God,*

Walking in Faith: Finding Peace, Strength, and Purpose On Your Journey

which transcends all understanding, will guard your hearts and your minds in Christ Jesus."

No matter where you are in life right now, you can experience deep and lasting contentment. Keep your heart anchored in faith, and watch how God fills you with peace beyond measure.

You are right where you are meant to be—trust the process and embrace the journey.

CHAPTER 4 - LIVING A LIFE OF LOVE, JOY, AND GRATITUDE

- Living with Joy and Gratitude
- Understanding God's Perfect Love: A Love That Transforms and Unites
- How to Live at Peace with Others
- Your Victory is Secured by Your Faith
- How to Become More Peaceful by Trusting in God's Promises
- Choosing Peace
- Your Victory is Secured by Your Faith
- Shifting Your Focus: From Loss to Blessings

Walking in Faith: Finding Peace, Strength, and Purpose On Your Journey

A life rooted in love, joy, and gratitude is a life that reflects the very nature of God. This chapter explores how embracing these qualities transforms our hearts, strengthens our faith, and brings us into deeper alignment with His purpose for us. True joy and peace do not come from external circumstances but from an unwavering trust in God's goodness and love.

A key part of living a life of love is learning how to live at peace with others. The world often promotes division, but God calls us to be peacemakers. Whether in our relationships, communities, or even within ourselves, choosing peace over conflict allows us to walk in harmony with God's will. Forgiveness, understanding, and humility are essential in fostering true peace.

Faith is the foundation of our victory, and we are reminded that our victory is secured by our faith. No matter what trials we face, we can stand firm in the assurance that God has already won the battle for us. Faith enables us to trust in His promises and walk in confidence, knowing that He is always working on our behalf.

This chapter is an invitation to embrace the abundant life God has called us to—a life filled with love that heals, joy that strengthens, and gratitude that transforms. By choosing to walk in these truths daily, we reflect the light of Christ and experience the fullness of His presence in our lives.

Living with Joy and Gratitude

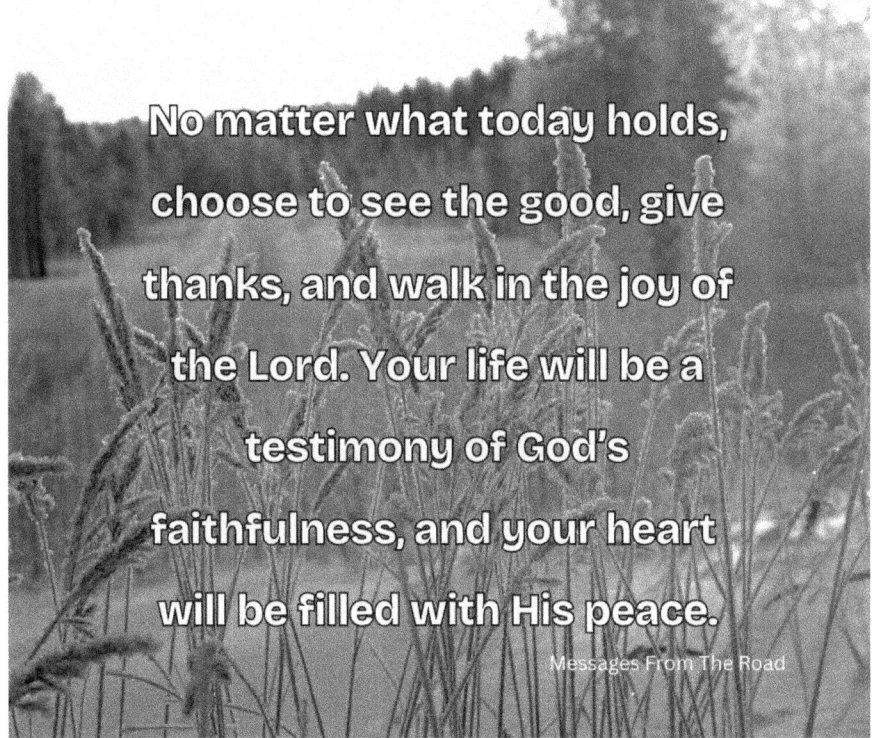

Life is full of ups and downs, but as believers, we are called to **rejoice always and give thanks in all circumstances**. This is not just a suggestion but a command from God, as stated in **1 Thessalonians 5:16-18**: *"Rejoice always, pray continually, give thanks in all circumstances; for this is God's will for you in Christ Jesus."*

Choosing to live with **joy and gratitude** transforms our outlook, strengthens our faith, and allows us to experience the peace that comes from trusting in God's perfect plan. No matter what happens—whether good or challenging—there is always a reason to **praise, trust, and give thanks**.

Living joyfully does not mean ignoring hardships or pretending that pain does not exist. Instead, it means anchoring ourselves in the unshakable truth that **God is always working for our good (Romans 8:28)**.

Tips for Choosing Faith Over Fear

By shifting our perspective, focusing on God's blessings, and choosing faith over fear, we can cultivate a heart that overflows with joy and thanksgiving in every season of life. Here's how you can do just that:

1. Focus on God's Promises, Not Your Problems

Difficulties will come, but what we focus on determines how we experience life. When we fix our hearts on God's promises rather than our problems, our perspective shifts from despair to hope.

- *"You will keep in perfect peace those whose minds are steadfast, because they trust in you."* — **Isaiah 26:3**
- *"I have told you these things, so that in me you may have peace. In this world you will have trouble. But take heart! I have overcome the world."* — **John 16:33**

Action Step: Start each day by reading a scripture that reminds you of God's faithfulness. When difficulties arise, replace negative thoughts with His promises.

2. Develop a Daily Habit of Gratitude

Gratitude is a powerful weapon against negativity and discouragement. By intentionally recognizing and thanking God for His blessings, we train our hearts to **see His goodness in every situation**.

- *"Give thanks to the Lord, for he is good; his love endures forever."* — **Psalm 107:1**
- *"Let them give thanks to the Lord for his unfailing love and his wonderful deeds for mankind."* — **Psalm 107:8**

Action Step: Keep a gratitude journal and write down at least three things you're thankful for each day. Speak out your gratitude in prayer, even in difficult moments.

3. Choose Joy as an Act of Faith

Joy is not dependent on circumstances; it is a choice and a fruit of the Spirit (**Galatians 5:22**). When we trust God and rejoice despite our situations, we reflect His light to the world.

- *"Consider it pure joy, my brothers and sisters, whenever you face trials of many kinds, because you know that the testing of your faith produces perseverance."* — **James 1:2-3**
- *"The joy of the Lord is your strength."* — **Nehemiah 8:10**

Action Step: When facing trials, **choose to worship instead of worry**. Sing a praise song, pray, or remind yourself of how God has been faithful in the past.

4. Serve Others and Spread Joy

One of the best ways to experience joy is by **bringing joy to others**. Serving, encouraging, and loving those around us helps shift our focus from our struggles to the blessings we can share.

- *"A generous person will prosper; whoever refreshes others will be refreshed."* — **Proverbs 11:25**
- *"Carry each other's burdens, and in this way, you will fulfill the law of Christ."* — **Galatians 6:2**

Action Step: Look for ways to bless someone each day—whether through kind words, acts of service, or simply sharing a smile.

5. Trust God's Plan and Timing

True joy comes when we **release control and trust that God is working behind the scenes**. Even when we don't understand why something is happening, we can rest knowing that God's plans are always for our good.

- *"Trust in the Lord with all your heart and lean not on your own understanding; in all your ways submit to him, and he will make your paths straight."* — **Proverbs 3:5-6**
- *"Be still, and know that I am God."* — **Psalm 46:10**

Action Step: When you feel anxious or frustrated, **pause and pray**. Surrender your worries to God and remind yourself that His timing is perfect.

Final Thought:

Living with **joy and gratitude** is a daily choice that brings freedom, peace, and deep fulfillment. When we focus on God's promises, cultivate gratitude, choose joy in all circumstances, serve others, and trust God's plan, we align ourselves with **His will for our lives**.

As **Philippians 4:4** reminds us, *"Rejoice in the Lord always. I will say it again: Rejoice!"* No matter what today holds, choose to **see the good, give thanks, and walk in the joy of the Lord**. Your life will be a testimony of God's faithfulness, and your heart will be filled with His peace.

Rejoice always, for God is good!

Understanding God's Perfect Love: A Love That Transforms and Unites

In a world often divided by differences, fear, and misunderstanding, God's perfect love stands as the unshakable force that binds us together. His love is not selective, conditional, or based on human standards—it is limitless, pure, and powerful. **1 John 4:18** reminds us, *"There is no fear in love. But perfect love drives out fear."*

This is the kind of love that allows us to overcome hate, embrace those different from us, and serve others selflessly. It is not a love rooted in emotions or circumstances, but in a deep understanding of God's nature and His command for us to love one another.

God's love is not measured by worldly success, outward appearances, or public approval. It is revealed in how we treat and care for others, especially the least among us. Jesus demonstrated this love—He dined with sinners, healed the outcasts, and forgave those who wronged Him.

His love is not just a feeling, but an action, a way of living that seeks the good of others above self-interest. **John 13:34-35** says, *"A new command I give you: Love one another. As I have loved you, so you must love one another. By this everyone will know that you are my disciples, if you love one another."*

Steps to Developing a Greater Understanding of God's Perfect Love

So how can we develop a deeper understanding of this love? How do we learn to love as God loves—beyond personal preferences, beyond social barriers, beyond conditions? Below are practical steps to help you grow in God's perfect love, a love that transforms hearts and brings healing to the world.

1. Seek to Know God More Deeply

To understand God's love, we must first know Him. Spend time in His Word, meditate on His character, and seek Him in prayer.

1 John 4:8 tells us, *"Whoever does not love does not know God, because God is love."*

The more we grow in relationship with Him, the more we will experience and reflect His perfect love.

2. Recognize That Love is a Choice, Not Just a Feeling

God's love is not based on fleeting emotions—it is a deliberate act of kindness, compassion, and sacrifice.

Romans 5:8 says, *"But God demonstrates His own love for us in this: While we were still sinners, Christ died for us."*

We are called to love even when it's difficult, even when people don't deserve it, because that is how God loves us.

3. Learn to See People Through God's Eyes

It's easy to love those who think and act like us, but true love embraces those who are different.

Jesus called us to love not just our friends, but even our enemies (**Luke 6:27-28**).

Ask God to help you see others as He does—not by their status, race, past, or appearance, but as His beloved children, worthy of grace.

4. Serve Others with a Selfless Heart

Love is best expressed through action. Jesus washed His disciples' feet, fed the hungry, and healed the sick—He showed love through service.

Galatians 5:13 says, *"Serve one another humbly in love."*

Look for ways to care for those in need, not for recognition, but to reflect God's love.

5. Forgive as You Have Been Forgiven

Love cannot thrive where resentment lives. God's love is full of mercy, and He calls us to extend that same grace to others.

Colossians 3:13 reminds us, *"Bear with each other and forgive one another if any of you has a grievance against someone. Forgive as the Lord forgave you."*

Letting go of grudges allows God's love to flow through us more freely.

6. Love Without Expecting Anything in Return

The world often teaches that love should be transactional—"I love you if you love me back." But God's love is unconditional.

Luke 6:35 says, *"But love your enemies, do good to them, and lend to them without expecting to get anything back. Then your reward will be great, and you will be children of the Most High."*

Love purely, without looking for something in return.

7. Let the Holy Spirit Guide You in Love

On our own, loving as God loves is impossible—but with the Holy Spirit, we can be transformed.

Romans 5:5 tells us, *"God's love has been poured out into our hearts through the Holy Spirit."*

Ask God daily to fill you with His love so that it naturally overflows to others.

Final Thought:

True love is not about what we get but about what we give. It is not defined by how people treat us, but by how we choose to love them regardless. God's perfect love drives out hate, fear, and division, replacing them with unity, kindness, and grace.

1 Corinthians 13:4-7 describes this love: *"Love is patient, love is kind... It always protects, always trusts, always hopes, always perseveres."*

As we grow in God's love, we become vessels of His grace—loving beyond barriers, serving without conditions, and forgiving without hesitation. Let this love define who you are, and let it be the light that draws others closer to Him. Because when we love as God loves, we reflect the very heart of Christ to the world.

How to Live at Peace with Others

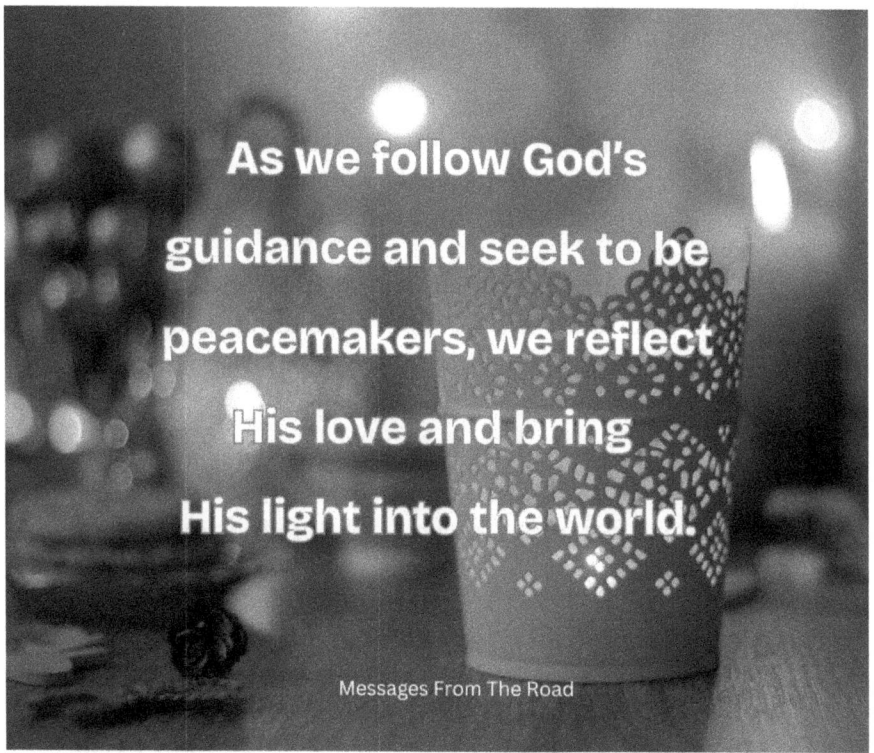

Living at peace with others is not always easy, but it is a calling that God has placed upon us. In a world filled with differences in opinions, backgrounds, and personalities, choosing understanding, love, and acceptance can transform our relationships and bring harmony into our lives.

Tips for Cultivating Peace With Those Around Us

The Bible provides clear guidance on how to cultivate peace with those around us. Here are key ways to live in peace, supported by scripture.

1. Practice Humility and Patience

Pride and impatience often lead to conflict, but humility allows us to listen and understand others better. When we are patient and humble, we create an environment where peace can flourish.

- *"Be completely humble and gentle; be patient, bearing with one another in love."* — **Ephesians 4:2**
- *"Do nothing out of selfish ambition or vain conceit. Rather, in humility value others above yourselves."* — **Philippians 2:3**

Action Step: Make a conscious effort to listen more than you speak, seek to understand before responding, and practice patience even in frustrating situations.

2. Love Others Unconditionally

Love is the foundation of peace. When we approach others with genuine love, we break down walls of division and build strong relationships.

- *"Above all, love each other deeply, because love covers over a multitude of sins."* — **1 Peter 4:8**
- *"A new command I give you: Love one another. As I have loved you, so you must love one another."* — **John 13:34**

Action Step: Show acts of kindness without expecting anything in return. Choose to love even when it's difficult, and let go of grudges that hinder peace.

3. Be a Peacemaker, Not a Troublemaker

We have the power to either promote peace or stir up conflict through our words and actions. God calls us to be peacemakers in all our interactions.

- *"Blessed are the peacemakers, for they will be called children of God."* — **Matthew 5:9**
- *"If it is possible, as far as it depends on you, live at peace with everyone."* — **Romans 12:18**

Action Step: Avoid gossip, unnecessary arguments, and harsh words. Instead, seek ways to mediate conflicts and encourage harmony.

4. Forgive Quickly and Let Go of Offenses

Holding onto grudges creates tension and bitterness, but forgiveness brings freedom and peace. Just as God forgives us, we are called to forgive others.

- *"Bear with each other and forgive one another if any of you has a grievance against someone. Forgive as the Lord forgave you."* — **Colossians 3:13**
- *"Get rid of all bitterness, rage and anger, brawling and slander, along with every form of malice."* — **Ephesians 4:31**

Action Step: When someone offends you, choose to let go rather than dwell on the hurt. Pray for the strength to forgive and move forward with peace in your heart.

5. Speak Words of Encouragement and Grace

Our words have the power to build up or tear down. Speaking with kindness and grace fosters understanding and strengthens relationships.

- *"Let your conversation be always full of grace, seasoned with salt, so that you may know how to answer everyone."* — **Colossians 4:6**
- *"A gentle answer turns away wrath, but a harsh word stirs up anger."* — **Proverbs 15:1**

Action Step: Think before you speak, choosing words that uplift rather than discourage. Offer encouragement and express appreciation to those around you.

6. Seek Understanding and Accept Differences

Everyone has unique experiences, perspectives, and struggles. Rather than allowing differences to divide us, we should seek to understand and accept one another.

- *"Accept one another, then, just as Christ accepted you, in order to bring praise to God." —* Romans 15:7
- *"Do to others as you would have them do to you." —* Luke 6:31

Action Step: Be open-minded and willing to see things from another person's point of view. Respect differences and look for common ground rather than focusing on what separates you.

7. Trust God to Work Through Difficult Relationships

Sometimes, despite our best efforts, peace seems impossible. In those moments, we must trust God to bring reconciliation and transformation.

- *"Cast all your anxiety on him because he cares for you." —* **1 Peter 5:7**
- *"The Lord gives strength to his people; the Lord blesses his people with peace." —* **Psalm 29:11**

Action Step: Pray for those you struggle to get along with and ask God for wisdom in handling difficult relationships. Trust that He is at work behind the scenes.

Final Thought:

Living at peace with others is a choice that requires effort, but it brings immeasurable blessings. Through humility, love, patience, and forgiveness, we can create harmony in our relationships.

As we follow God's guidance and seek to be peacemakers, we reflect His love and bring His light into the world. May we all strive to live in peace, understanding, and acceptance, just as Christ has shown us. *"Let us therefore make every effort to do what leads to peace and to mutual edification."* — **Romans 14:19**

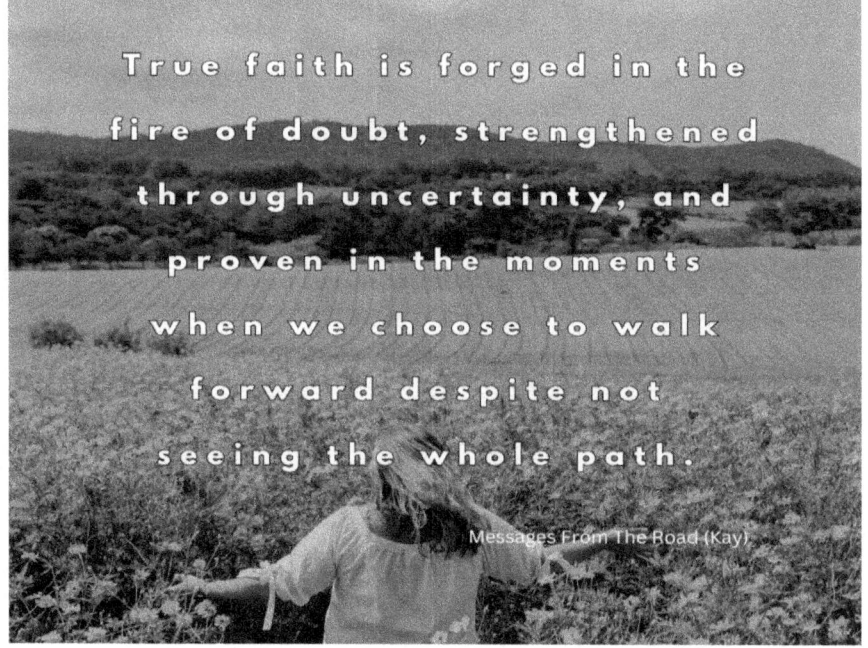

How To Become More Peaceful by Trusting in God's Promises

> Resting assuredly in God's promises is a journey of faith and daily surrender. As we commit to trusting Him, we'll find peace, hope, and joy that cannot be shaken by circumstances.
>
> Messages From The Road

Resting assuredly in God's promises brings a peace that surpasses all understanding. When we rest in His promises, we lean into a trust that doesn't waver with changing circumstances, knowing that God's Word is unshakeable. His promises are a firm foundation, rooted in love, grace, and the assurance of His presence.

When life feels uncertain, we can remember His words in **Jeremiah 29:11**, "For I know the plans I have for you, plans to prosper you and not to harm you, plans to give you hope and a future." In resting assuredly, we allow God's promises to quiet our doubts and calm our fears.

How to Trust in God's Promises

Trusting in God's promises means building a deep trust in His Word, even when we cannot see the way ahead. Here are some steps to help you trust in God's promises with confidence and peace:

1. Know His Promises

Spend time reading the Bible and familiarizing yourself with God's promises. Passages like **Jeremiah 29:11**, **Isaiah 41:10**, and **Romans 8:28** remind us of His faithfulness, plans, and love. The more we know His Word, the easier it becomes to trust it.

2. Pray with Faith

Prayer strengthens our connection to God and reminds us of His power and love. Pour out your worries and hopes to Him, and trust that He hears you. Prayer helps turn our focus from our anxieties to God's power and presence.

3. Reflect on Past Faithfulness

Remember times when God came through in your life or others'. Reflecting on His past faithfulness can strengthen your confidence in His promises for the present and future.

4. Practice Gratitude

Being grateful, even during uncertain times, helps cultivate a trusting heart. Each day, thank God for His blessings and the small ways you see His love. Gratitude shifts our perspective to one of faith rather than worry.

5. Surround Yourself with Encouragement

Spend time with others who share your faith and encourage one another with God's Word. Fellowship can remind us that we're not alone and that others are also resting in His promises.

6. Release Control

Trusting God sometimes means releasing our need for control and surrendering the outcome to Him. We can let go, knowing that He is working all things for good (**Romans 8:28**) and that His timing is perfect.

7. Claim His Promises Daily

Each day, speak God's promises over your life. Even during challenges, say them out loud to remind yourself that God is faithful. Words have power, and affirming His promises can strengthen our resolve to trust in them.

Final Thought:

Resting assuredly in God's promises is a journey of faith and daily surrender. As we commit to trusting Him, we'll find peace, hope, and joy that cannot be shaken by circumstances.

So let us surrender our worries and rest in His promises today, confident that He is working all things for our good. Let Go and Let God.

Choosing Peace

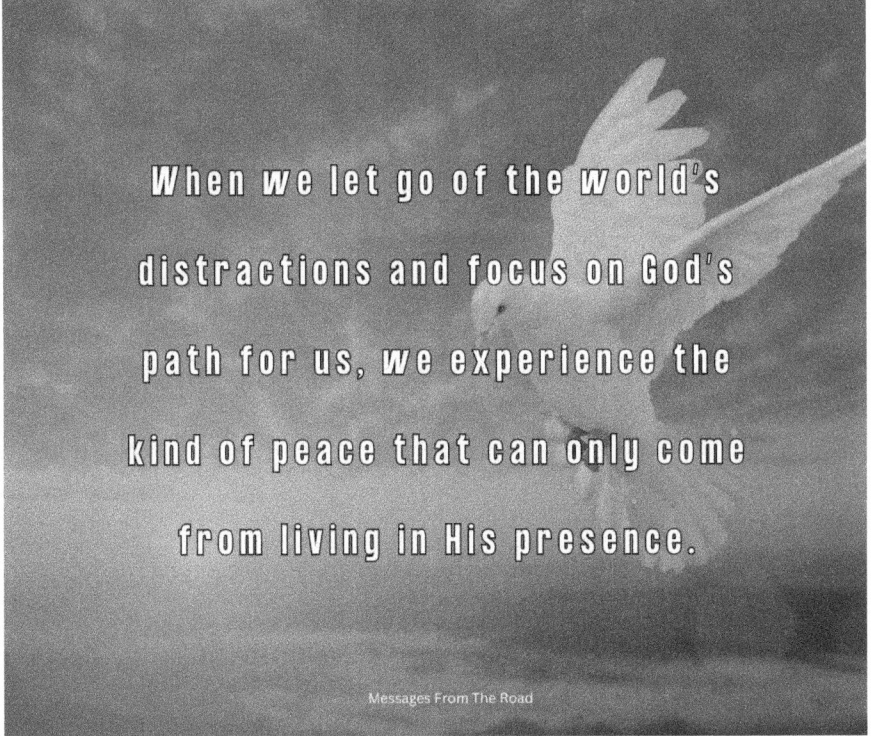

In a world filled with chaos, conflict, and distractions, choosing peace and walking in God's ways can often feel like a difficult path to follow. The brokenness of this fallen world constantly pulls at us, tempting us to respond with fear, anger, or despair. However, God's Word reminds us that peace is not something we achieve through circumstances—it's a gift we receive when we align our hearts with His will.

Walking in God's ways brings clarity, strength, and a sense of purpose that transcends the challenges we face. It's not always easy, but when we choose to seek Him, we open the door to a peace that surpasses all understanding.

How to Choose Peace Over Conflict

1. Anchor Yourself in God's Word

God's Word serves as our guide, teaching us how to live in peace and righteousness even in a troubled world. Regular meditation on Scripture helps you align your thoughts and actions with His will. *"Great peace have those who love your law, and nothing can make them stumble."* — **Psalm 119:165**

How To:

- Start your day with a Bible verse or passage that encourages peace and trust.
- Reflect on how you can apply God's teachings to your daily challenges.

2. Choose Peace Through Prayer

Prayer is a powerful way to surrender your worries and align your heart with God's peace. It helps you to focus on His promises rather than your circumstances.

"Do not be anxious about anything, but in every situation, by prayer and petition, with thanksgiving, present your requests to God. And the peace of God, which transcends all understanding, will guard your hearts and your minds in Christ Jesus." — **Philippians 4:6-7**

How To:

- When you feel overwhelmed, pause and pray, asking for God's guidance and peace.
- Cultivate a habit of gratitude in prayer, which shifts your focus from problems to blessings.

3. Let the Holy Spirit Guide You

God's Spirit within us helps us discern the right path and equips us with the fruit of peace. Allowing the Holy Spirit to lead you means letting go of control and trusting God's wisdom. *"The mind governed by the Spirit is life and peace."* — **Romans 8:6**

How To:

- Take time in silence to listen for God's voice and direction.
- Ask the Holy Spirit to guide your responses, especially in challenging situations.

4. Practice Forgiveness and Let Go of Resentment

Carrying anger or unforgiveness disrupts our peace and distances us from God's ways. Choosing to forgive as God forgives us brings freedom and restores harmony. *"Bear with each other and forgive one another if any of you has a grievance against someone. Forgive as the Lord forgave you."* — **Colossians 3:13**

How To:

- Identify areas where resentment is holding you back and pray for the strength to forgive.
- Remember that forgiveness doesn't excuse wrongdoing but frees your heart to heal.

5. Focus on What Is Good and Noble

Our thoughts shape our emotions and actions. Choosing to focus on things that are pure and admirable helps us maintain peace in our hearts.
"Finally, brothers and sisters, whatever is true, whatever is noble, whatever is right, whatever is pure, whatever is lovely, whatever is admirable—if anything is excellent or praiseworthy—think about such things." — **Philippians 4:8**

How To:

- Reframe negative thoughts by focusing on God's blessings and promises.

- Surround yourself with uplifting influences, such as positive people and encouraging content.

6. Trust in God's Sovereignty

Peace comes when we trust that God is in control, even when life feels uncertain. Surrendering to His sovereignty allows us to rest in His perfect plan.
"You will keep in perfect peace those whose minds are steadfast, because they trust in you." — **Isaiah 26:3**

How To:

- Remind yourself daily that God is working all things for your good.
- Reflect on past situations where God's faithfulness brought you through challenges.

Final Thought:

Choosing peace and walking in God's ways requires intentionality, but it leads to a life of fulfillment, joy, and a deeper connection with Him. When we let go of the world's distractions and focus on His path, we experience the kind of peace that can only come from living in His presence.

His path leads to peace, strength, and victory. Trust that He has already won the battles ahead of you, and rest in the confidence that His power is working through you.

"The Lord your God is with you, the Mighty Warrior who saves. He will take great delight in you; in His love He will no longer rebuke you but will rejoice over you with singing." — **Zephaniah 3:17**

Your Victory is Secured by Your Faith

"Faith Is Your Victory" is a powerful reminder that true strength and victory come from unwavering trust in God. Faith isn't just hope for a better outcome; it's the confident assurance that God is working behind the scenes, aligning every detail for our good and His glory.

1 John 5:4 tells us, *"This is the victory that has overcome the world—our faith."* This means that no matter the challenges or trials we face, our faith gives us the victory to overcome.

Faith isn't the absence of difficulties; it's the courage to stand firm despite them. It's believing that even in the darkest moments, God is by our side, leading us toward His perfect plan.

Faith allows us to see beyond the present and trust in God's promises, knowing that He is with us every step of the way. With faith, we gain strength to press on, peace in our waiting, and hope that endures.

Ways to Cultivate and Strengthen Your Faith

Growing your faith is a journey that deepens your relationship with God, strengthens your trust in His promises, and empowers you to live with peace, joy, and purpose. Here are some practical ways to cultivate and strengthen your faith:

1. Spend Time in God's Word

- **Read the Bible Regularly**: The Bible is filled with promises, truths, and stories of God's faithfulness. Start with passages that speak to you or find a reading plan to help guide your study.
- **Meditate on Scripture**: Take time to really dwell on specific verses, letting God's truth fill your heart and mind. Memorize verses like **Proverbs 3:5-6** and **Hebrews 11:1** to reinforce your trust in Him.

2. Pray Continually and Honestly

- **Be Transparent with God**: Talk to Him about your doubts, struggles, and desires. Building a consistent prayer life invites God into every area of your life and builds trust.
- **Listen for His Guidance**: Prayer is a two-way conversation. Take time to quiet your mind and listen for God's gentle nudges, letting His voice guide your steps and strengthen your faith.

3. Put Your Faith Into Action

- **Step Out in Obedience**: Trusting God sometimes means stepping out of your comfort zone. Even small acts of faith in obedience to His call help your faith grow.

- **Serve Others**: When we serve, we learn to trust in God's provision and experience His love in action. Acts of kindness and selflessness are ways to live out our faith practically.

4. Surround Yourself with Faith-Building Community

- **Join a Faith Group or Church**: Being part of a community, like our Messages From The Road group, where others encourage and share testimonies of God's faithfulness, can strengthen your faith. Surround yourself with people who will uplift you in prayer and remind you of God's promises.
- **Seek Mentorship**: A trusted mentor can offer guidance, wisdom, and accountability as you grow. They can share their experiences of faith and help you navigate challenges.

5. Practice Gratitude and Worship

- **Thank God Daily**: Gratitude shifts our focus from worries to blessings, reminding us of God's faithfulness in our lives. Regularly thanking God reinforces our trust in Him.
- **Worship from the Heart**: Worship connects us deeply with God and helps us focus on His greatness. Worship, even in hard times, strengthens our faith and invites His presence into our lives.

6. Remember and Reflect on God's Faithfulness

- **Keep a Faith Journal**: Write down answered prayers, moments of encouragement, or scriptures that inspire you. Reflecting on God's past faithfulness reminds you that He is always working in your life.
- **Celebrate Small Steps of Growth**: Every step, no matter how small, is a sign that God is working in you. Celebrating growth in your faith encourages you to keep going.

7. Trust in His Timing and Plan

- **Wait with Patience and Hope**: Faith grows in times of waiting, as we learn to rely on God's timing rather than our own. Trust that He sees the big picture, even when we cannot.
- **Release Control to God**: Letting go of the need to control every outcome opens the door for God's power to work in your life. By surrendering to His plan, you acknowledge that He is in control and trustworthy.

Final Thought:

When life feels uncertain, remember that your victory is already secured by your faith. It's a victory that conquers fear, silences doubt, and invites God's miraculous power into your life.

Stand firm in this faith and trust that God is fighting for you, and that in Him, you are more than a conqueror. Faith is your victory—hold onto it, and let it guide you through every season.

Shifting Your Focus: From Loss to Blessings

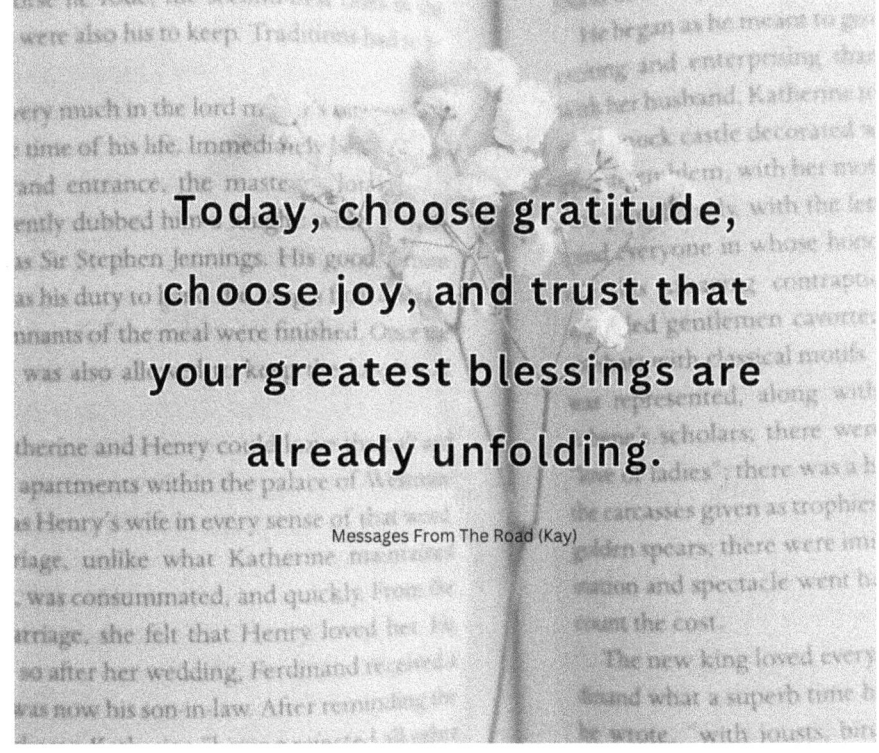

Today, choose gratitude, choose joy, and trust that your greatest blessings are already unfolding.

Messages From The Road (Kay)

In life, it's easy to focus on what we've lost, what we lack, or what hasn't gone as planned. Disappointments, setbacks, and hardships can weigh heavily on our hearts, making it difficult to see the good that still surrounds us. However, true peace and joy come when we shift our perspective—**choosing gratitude over lack, contentment over comparison, and trust over doubt.**

God calls us to focus not on what is missing, but on **His abundant blessings, His presence, and His promises.** *"Give thanks in all circumstances; for this is God's will for you in Christ Jesus."* (**1 Thessalonians 5:18**). When we intentionally shift our focus from loss to gratitude, we begin to see **how much we still have and how much God is still doing in our lives.**

Steps to Shift Your Focus to Your Blessings

It's easy to focus on what we don't have or what is missing. To do as God wishes, and focus on gratitude can be challenging. Here are steps to help you shift your focus to your blessings:

1. Start Each Day with Gratitude

Instead of dwelling on what you lack, begin your day by thanking God for what you do have. Take a moment to list at least **three blessings**—your health, loved ones, a new day, or even something as simple as the air you breathe.

"This is the day that the Lord has made; let us rejoice and be glad in it." – **Psalm 118:24**

2. Meditate on God's Promises, Not Your Problems

God has promised to take care of you, even when things feel uncertain. When negative thoughts arise, replace them with scripture and **remind yourself of God's faithfulness.**

"And my God will supply every need of yours according to His riches in glory in Christ Jesus." – **Philippians 4:19**

3. Shift Your Perspective from "Why Me?" to "What Can I Learn?"

Instead of asking, *"Why did this happen to me?"* ask, *"What is God teaching me through this?"* Often, our greatest growth comes from our struggles.

"We know that in all things God works for the good of those who love Him, who have been called according to His purpose." – **Romans 8:28**

4. Keep a Blessings Journal

Each evening, write down **at least three things that brought you joy or peace** during the day. Over time, you'll see that even in the hardest seasons, **God has never stopped blessing you.**

5. Help and Serve Others

One of the best ways to shift your focus from what's missing to what's present is by **helping someone else.** When you bless others, you begin to see the abundance in your own life.

"It is more blessed to give than to receive." – **Acts 20:35**

6. Let Go and Trust God's Plan

Sometimes, we don't understand why things happen, but we can **trust that God is still in control.** Choose to surrender your worries and believe that He has something greater ahead.

"Trust in the Lord with all your heart and lean not on your own understanding; in all your ways submit to Him, and He will make your paths straight." – **Proverbs 3:5-6**

Final Thought:

Shifting your focus from **what you lack to what you have** is a daily practice, but one that brings **peace, joy, and a renewed sense of purpose.** When you start seeing life through the lens of gratitude, you will realize that **even in the hardest moments, God is still good, and His blessings still surround you.**

Instead of looking at what's missing, **embrace what's present.** Instead of longing for what was, **trust in what's ahead.** And most importantly, **believe that God's love, grace, and provision are more than enough for you.**

CHAPTER 5 - SPIRITUAL TRANSFORMATION AND GROWTH

- Transforming Yourself by Living in the Spirit of God
- Developing Self-Belief, Trusting the Process, and Enjoying the Journey
- Transforming Doubt and Fear into Deeper Faith and Trust
- Staying Mindful of God In Every Situation and Seeing Life From His Perspective
- How to Be Like Jesus While on This Earth
- Learning to Trust God in Times of Distress and Growing in Character

**Walking in Faith: Finding Peace, Strength, and Purpose
On Your Journey**

Spiritual transformation is a lifelong journey of becoming more like Christ. It is not about striving for perfection but about allowing God to shape us through His Spirit, guiding us into deeper faith, trust, and purpose. This chapter explores how to surrender to the Holy Spirit's work in our lives, letting go of fear and doubt and embracing a life of faith, confidence, and divine guidance.

A key part of this transformation is **overcoming fear and doubt, replacing them with faith and trust.** Fear keeps us stagnant, but faith propels us forward. Through scripture and personal reflection, we explore how to let go of anxiety and walk in the boldness of God's promises.

To truly grow spiritually, we must also learn to **stay mindful of God in every situation and see life from His perspective.** Instead of reacting to challenges with worry, we can develop the habit of seeing them through the lens of faith—understanding that God is always at work, even when we cannot see the full picture. This mindset shift brings peace and clarity, allowing us to walk in alignment with His will.

Spiritual growth is an ongoing process, but when we commit to walking in the Spirit, trusting God's plan, and embracing transformation, we step into the fullness of the life He has designed for us. This chapter will guide you toward a deeper, more fulfilling relationship with God, equipping you to walk in faith, love, and purpose.

Transforming Yourself by Living in the Spirit of God

Many people struggle with overthinking, fear, and uncertainty, relying on their own understanding instead of fully surrendering to the Spirit of God.

However, true transformation happens when we shift from living in our own minds—filled with doubt and human limitations—to living by the power and guidance of the Holy Spirit.

When we walk in the Spirit, we experience peace, wisdom, strength, and a deep connection with God's purpose for our lives.

Romans 8:5-6 reminds us, *"For those who live according to the flesh set their minds on the things of the flesh, but those who live according to the Spirit set their minds on the things of the Spirit. For to set the mind on the flesh is death, but to set the mind on the Spirit is life and peace."*

Steps for Living in the Spirit of God

To step into the fullness of the Spirit and live the life you were meant to live, here are key steps to guide you on this journey:

1. Surrender Your Mind to God

Transformation begins with surrender. Let go of the need to control every outcome and place your trust in God's wisdom.

Proverbs 3:5-6 says, *"Trust in the Lord with all your heart, and do not lean on your own understanding. In all your ways acknowledge Him, and He will make straight your paths."*

Action: Instead of relying on logic alone, invite the Holy Spirit to guide your decisions and thoughts.

2. Renew Your Mind Through the Word

Your mind must be renewed daily with God's truth.

Romans 12:2 instructs us, *"Do not be conformed to this world, but be transformed by the renewal of your mind, that by testing you may discern what is the will of God, what is good and acceptable and perfect."*

Action: Meditate on Scripture, spend time in God's presence, and allow His truth to replace fear, doubt, and negativity.

3. Walk by the Spirit, Not the Flesh

Living in the Spirit means making daily choices that align with God's ways rather than worldly desires.

Galatians 5:16 says, *"Walk by the Spirit, and you will not gratify the desires of the flesh."*

Action: The more we choose righteousness over sin, faith over fear, and love over selfishness, the more we align with the Spirit's leading.

4. Develop a Deep Prayer Life

Prayer is the gateway to spiritual intimacy with God. Instead of overthinking, take everything to Him in prayer.

Philippians 4:6-7 reminds us, *"Do not be anxious about anything, but in everything by prayer and supplication with thanksgiving let your requests be made known to God. And the peace of God, which surpasses all understanding, will guard your hearts and your minds in Christ Jesus."*

Action: Prayer transforms your thoughts and aligns you with the Spirit.

5. Listen for the Holy Spirit's Voice

God speaks in stillness. If you're always relying on your own thoughts, you may miss His direction.

John 16:13 says, *"When the Spirit of truth comes, He will guide you into all the truth."*

Action: Spend quiet time with God, listen for His voice, and trust the promptings of the Holy Spirit.

6. Live by Faith, Not Feelings

Faith in God means trusting even when you don't understand everything.

2 Corinthians 5:7 reminds us, *"For we walk by faith, not by sight."*

Action: Don't let emotions dictate your actions—let God's truth be your foundation.

7. Bear the Fruit of the Spirit

A life led by the Spirit reflects God's love, peace, and righteousness.

Galatians 5:22-23 describes the fruit of the Spirit as *"love, joy, peace, patience, kindness, goodness, faithfulness, gentleness, self-control."*

Action: When you live by the Spirit, your life becomes a testimony of God's goodness.

Final Thought:

Living in the Spirit is a daily journey of surrender, faith, and transformation. When you shift your focus from your own thoughts to God's presence, you will experience a life of **purpose, peace, and divine guidance.** As you let the Spirit lead, you will step into the fullness of who God created you to be.

Romans 8:14 declares, *"For all who are led by the Spirit of God are sons of God."*

Let go of self-reliance, embrace the Spirit's leading, and walk boldly into the life God has designed for you. Trust Him completely, and watch as He transforms your heart, mind, and future.

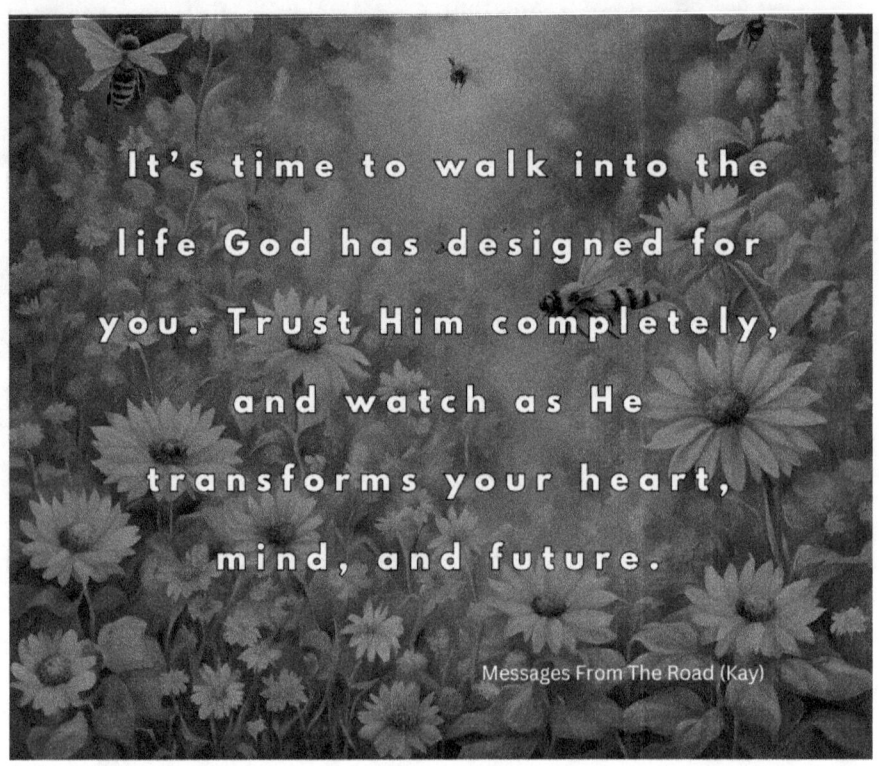

Developing Self-Belief, Trusting the Process, and Enjoying the Journey

Believing in yourself is the foundation of a fulfilling and successful life. However, self-doubt, fear of failure, and impatience can often make the journey feel overwhelming. Learning to trust the process and enjoy the path you're on is essential to personal growth.

Learning to Believe in Yourself

Life is not just about reaching a destination—it's about embracing the lessons, experiences, and moments that shape you along the way. **When you develop self-belief, surrender to the process, and find joy in the journey, you unlock the power to achieve anything you set your mind to.** Here's how to cultivate this mindset.

1. Cultivate a Positive Mindset

Your thoughts shape your reality. Replace self-doubt with affirmations and positive self-talk. Instead of saying, *"I'm not good enough,"* tell yourself, *"I am capable, strong, and growing every day."*

Proverbs 23:7 says, *"As a man thinks in his heart, so is he."*

Action: Fill your mind with thoughts that uplift and empower you.

2. Set Realistic Goals and Take Small Steps

Belief in yourself grows when you take action. Set small, achievable goals and celebrate your progress. Each step forward builds confidence and reinforces the belief that you are capable of success.

Philippians 4:13 reminds us, *"I can do all things through Christ who strengthens me."*

Action: Keep moving forward, one step at a time.

3. Embrace Challenges as Growth Opportunities

Difficulties are not roadblocks—they are lessons that make you stronger. Instead of fearing failure, see it as a stepping stone toward growth.

James 1:2-4 encourages us, *"Consider it pure joy, my brothers and sisters, whenever you face trials of many kinds, because you know that the testing of your faith produces perseverance."*

Action: Trust that every challenge is shaping you for something greater.

4. Trust That Everything is Working for Your Good

Even when things don't go as planned, trust that life is unfolding exactly as it should.

Romans 8:28 assures us, *"And we know that in all things God works for the good of those who love him."*

Action: Let go of the need to control every detail and believe that the process is leading you toward something amazing.

5. Practice Gratitude Daily

Joy is found in the present moment, not just in reaching a destination. Take time to appreciate where you are now, even as you work toward where you want to be.

1 Thessalonians 5:18 reminds us, *"Give thanks in all circumstances; for this is God's will for you in Christ Jesus."*

Action: Keep a gratitude journal or take a few moments each day to reflect on the blessings in your life.

6. Surround Yourself with Encouragement

Your environment plays a huge role in your self-belief.

Proverbs 27:17 says, *"As iron sharpens iron, so one person sharpens another."*

Action: Surround yourself with people who uplift, support, and inspire you. Find mentors, friends, or communities that encourage growth and remind you of your potential.

7. Enjoy the Journey—Not Just the Destination

Life is not a race; it's a journey to be enjoyed. Stop waiting for the "perfect" moment to be happy. The journey itself is shaping you into the person you are meant to be.

Action: Celebrate small victories, find joy in the process, and appreciate the beauty of where you are today.

Final Thought:

Self-belief, trust in the process, and enjoyment of the journey are not things you achieve overnight—they are built through daily choices and a mindset of faith and perseverance. When you choose to embrace challenges, take small steps forward, and find joy in every season, you begin to realize that everything is unfolding exactly as it should.

God is guiding your path, and your potential is limitless. Keep believing, keep trusting, and most importantly—keep enjoying the beautiful journey of becoming the best version of yourself.

Transforming Doubt & Fear into Deeper Faith & Trust

Keeping doubt and fear from silencing our faith is an ongoing journey, one that requires both inner strength and reliance on God's promises. By staying grounded in His Word and trusting in His character, we can transform doubt and fear into catalysts for deeper faith and resilience.

Ways to Cultivate Confidence and Hope, Even in the Face of Doubt

1. Anchor Yourself in God's Promises

Start by reminding yourself of the promises God has made and fulfilled throughout Scripture.

Verses like **Isaiah 41:10**—*"Do not fear, for I am with you; do not be dismayed, for I am your God. I will strengthen you and help you"*—reassure us that God's presence and power are steadfast.

Regularly reading and memorizing His promises will fill you with confidence, reminding you that you are never alone.

2. Pray for Strength and Peace

Bring your fears and doubts to God in prayer, asking Him to replace them with peace and confidence.

In **Philippians 4:6-7**, we're reminded to *"not be anxious about anything, but in every situation, by prayer and petition, with thanksgiving, present your requests to God. And the peace of God... will guard your hearts."*

Prayer invites God's presence to calm your mind and strengthen your faith.

3. Recall Times When God Has Been Faithful

Reflect on how God has come through for you in the past. Remembering these instances builds faith for future challenges.

Like the psalmist who wrote, *"I remember the days of long ago; I meditate on all your works"* (**Psalm 143:5**), looking back on God's faithfulness renews our hope and reminds us that He will come through again.

4. Speak Truth to Yourself

Combat doubt and fear by speaking truth over your life. Say, "God is with me. I am loved. I am capable."

Remind yourself of **2 Timothy 1:7**, which says, *"For God has not given us a spirit of fear, but of power and of love and of a sound mind."*

Speaking truth dispels the lies that doubt and fear can bring.

5. Choose Faith Over Feelings

Faith is an active choice, not a feeling. Doubts may come, but choose to focus on God's truth instead of your fears.

Proverbs 3:5-6 encourages us, *"Trust in the Lord with all your heart and lean not on your own understanding."*

Faith often requires moving forward, even when it feels uncertain, trusting that God will guide you each step of the way.

6. Stay Connected to Faith Community

Being part of a faith community provides support and encouragement. Surround yourself with people who remind you of God's love, pray with you, and encourage you to keep your faith strong.

Hebrews 10:24-25 says, *"And let us consider how we may spur one another on toward love and good deeds."*

Community keeps you accountable and hopeful.

7. Turn Doubts Into Growth Opportunities

View doubt not as a failure, but as a chance to deepen your relationship with God. Questioning and seeking truth can lead to stronger faith.

In **James 1:2-4**, we're reminded that *"the testing of your faith produces perseverance."*

Let doubt motivate you to draw closer to God, asking for clarity and reassurance.

8. Trust God's Timing and Plan

Often, fear arises from wanting immediate answers or control over outcomes. Surrendering your timeline to God brings peace, knowing His plan is greater than ours.

Jeremiah 29:11 assures us, *"For I know the plans I have for you," declares the Lord, "plans to prosper you and not to harm you, plans to give you hope and a future."*

Resting in this truth builds confidence and trust in His process.

9. Visualize the Outcome of Your Faith in Action

Imagine the rewards of staying faithful and hopeful: a stronger relationship with God, peace, and resilience in the face of adversity.

Hebrews 11:1 reminds us, *"Now faith is confidence in what we hope for and assurance about what we do not see."*

Seeing faith's impact on your life motivates you to trust and hold onto hope.

Final Thought:

By practicing these nine things on a consistent basis, you will see your life transform and doubt and fear being replaced by a deeper faith and resilience.

Staying Mindful of God in Every Situation & Seeing Life from His Perspective

In the busyness of life, it's easy to get caught up in daily challenges, distractions, and emotions. We often react to situations based on our immediate feelings rather than pausing to seek God's wisdom. Yet, true peace and clarity come when we align our thoughts with His and see life through His eyes.

Staying mindful of God in every situation helps us navigate life with greater faith, patience, and trust. It allows us to experience His presence more deeply and make decisions that reflect His will.

"Set your minds on things above, not on earthly things." — **Colossians 3:2**

How to Cultivate Awareness of God Throughout Your Day

Here are practical ways to cultivate awareness of God throughout your day and develop the ability to see things from His divine perspective.

1. Begin Each Day with God

How we start our day often sets the tone for everything that follows. Taking time in the morning to pray, reflect, and seek God's presence helps keep our hearts and minds focused on Him.

"Let the morning bring me word of Your unfailing love, for I have put my trust in You." — **Psalm 143:8**

How to Apply It:

- Spend a few quiet moments in prayer before checking your phone or engaging with the world.
- Read a passage from the Bible and meditate on its meaning for your day.
- Ask God to guide your thoughts and actions throughout the day.

Benefit: Starting your day with God strengthens your spiritual awareness, helping you remain mindful of Him in every situation.

2. Invite God Into Every Moment

God is not just present in church or during prayer time—He is with us in every moment. When we invite Him into our daily routines, we cultivate an awareness of His presence in even the smallest details of life.

"In all your ways acknowledge Him, and He will make your paths straight." — **Proverbs 3:6**

How to Apply It:

- Say a short prayer before making decisions, big or small.
- Ask, *"God, what do You want me to see in this situation?"*
- Look for opportunities to show kindness, patience, or love as an act of worship.

Benefit: Acknowledging God throughout your day helps you align your thoughts and actions with His will.

3. Train Your Mind to See Through God's Perspective

When challenges arise, our natural response is often frustration, worry, or doubt. But when we pause to view situations through God's eyes, we gain wisdom and peace beyond our understanding.

"Do not conform to the pattern of this world, but be transformed by the renewing of your mind." — **Romans 12:2**

How to Apply It:

- When facing a problem, ask, *"How does God see this situation?"*
- Replace negative thoughts with His promises—focus on His truth rather than emotions.
- Trust that even difficulties have a purpose in God's plan.

Benefit: Seeing life from God's perspective reduces stress, builds faith, and helps you respond with wisdom rather than impulsiveness.

4. Slow Down & Practice Gratitude

One of the best ways to stay mindful of God is by slowing down and appreciating His blessings. A hurried life often leads to spiritual blindness, but gratitude opens our eyes to His goodness.

"Give thanks in all circumstances; for this is God's will for you in Christ Jesus." — **1 Thessalonians 5:18**

How to Apply It:

- Take moments throughout the day to pause, breathe, and thank God.
- Keep a gratitude journal to remind yourself of His blessings.
- Instead of focusing on what's wrong, recognize what God is doing right.

Benefit: Gratitude shifts your focus from problems to God's presence, bringing greater joy and contentment.

5. Surround Yourself with God's Truth

What we fill our minds with influences how we think and see the world. Immersing ourselves in God's Word and surrounding ourselves with uplifting influences helps keep our thoughts aligned with His.

"Your word is a lamp to my feet and a light for my path." — **Psalm 119:105**

How to Apply It:

- Listen to worship music or faith-based podcasts during your commute or free time.
- Read or memorize Bible verses that remind you of God's character and promises.
- Spend time with people who encourage you in faith.

Benefit: Filling your mind with God's truth strengthens your spiritual vision and deepens your connection with Him.

6. Surrender Worries & Trust His Plan

When we try to control everything, we often lose sight of God's sovereignty. Surrendering our fears and uncertainties to Him allows us to walk in faith rather than anxiety.

"Cast all your anxiety on Him because He cares for you." — **1 Peter 5:7**

How to Apply It:

- When worries arise, immediately pray and give them to God.
- Remember past times when God provided for you, and trust He will do it again.
- Rest in the truth that God is always in control, even when you don't understand.

Benefit: Surrendering to God brings peace and freedom from the burden of anxiety.

7. End Your Day in Reflection & Prayer

Just as beginning the day with God is important, ending it with Him allows us to reflect on His presence throughout the day. It also helps us rest in peace, knowing He holds everything in His hands.

"I will lie down and sleep in peace, for You alone, O Lord, make me dwell in safety." — **Psalm 4:8**

How to Apply It:

- Take a few minutes before bed to reflect on how you saw God working in your day.
- Confess anything that burdens your heart and ask for His peace.
- Thank Him for His presence, protection, and love.

Benefit: Ending your day with God strengthens your faith and allows you to rest in His peace.

Final Thought:

Living with a mindful awareness of God transforms how we experience life. By intentionally seeking Him in every situation, we begin to see the world through His perspective—one of hope, grace, and purpose. No matter what comes your way, remember: **God is always near, always guiding, and always working for your good.**

"The Lord Himself goes before you and will be with you; He will never leave you nor forsake you. Do not be afraid; do not be discouraged." — **Deuteronomy 31:8**

Make today a step toward greater mindfulness of God. The more you practice, the more naturally His presence will become the foundation of your life.

Make today a step toward greater mindfulness of God. The more you practice, the more naturally His presence will become the foundation of your life.

**Walking in Faith: Finding Peace, Strength, and Purpose
On Your Journey**

How to Be Like Jesus While on This Earth

Living a life modeled after Jesus Christ is both a profound calling and a daily journey of growth. While none of us can be perfect, striving to reflect Jesus' character allows us to live with purpose, love, and grace.

Principles for Striving to Be Like Jesus

Here are some principles to guide your path:

1. Walk in Love

Jesus taught us to love God and our neighbors above all else (**Matthew 22:37-39**). This love is selfless, compassionate, and unconditional. Look for opportunities to serve others, forgive freely, and extend kindness, even when it's difficult.

"A new command I give you: Love one another. As I have loved you, so you must love one another." – **John 13:34**

2. Embrace Humility

Jesus lived a life of humility, putting the needs of others before His own. Be willing to listen, learn, and serve without seeking recognition or praise. True greatness in God's kingdom is found in serving others.

"Whoever wants to become great among you must be your servant." – **Matthew 20:26**

3. Seek God's Will in All Things

Jesus consistently sought the will of His Father, spending time in prayer and obedience. Make prayer a daily habit and trust God's guidance in your decisions.

"Not my will, but yours be done." – **Luke 22:42**

4. Live a Life of Forgiveness

Jesus forgave those who wronged Him, even as He suffered on the cross. Let go of bitterness and resentment, choosing forgiveness as a way to reflect His grace.

"Father, forgive them, for they do not know what they are doing." – **Luke 23:34**

5. Be a Light to Others

Jesus called His followers to be the light of the world. Share your faith, spread hope, and be an example of goodness and integrity in your actions.

"Let your light shine before others, that they may see your good deeds and glorify your Father in heaven." – **Matthew 5:16**

6. Cultivate Compassion

Jesus healed the sick, comforted the brokenhearted, and cared for the marginalized. Open your heart to those in need and look for ways to bring healing and encouragement to others.

"When he saw the crowds, he had compassion on them." – **Matthew 9:36**

7. Grow in Faith and Knowledge

Jesus studied scripture and demonstrated an unwavering trust in God's promises. Immerse yourself in God's Word, grow in your faith, and apply His teachings to your daily life.

"Man shall not live on bread alone, but on every word that comes from the mouth of God." – **Matthew 4:4**

8. Persevere in Trials

Jesus endured suffering with courage and faith, trusting God's plan even in the face of great adversity. In your own challenges, lean on God for strength and remain steadfast in faith.

"In this world you will have trouble. But take heart! I have overcome the world." – **John 16:33**

Final Thought:

By aligning your thoughts, words, and actions with Jesus' example, you can live a life that honors God and transforms the world around you. Each step, no matter how small, brings you closer to reflecting His love and light.

Learning to Trust God in Times of Distress and Growing in Character

Life is full of challenges—unexpected setbacks, loss, uncertainty, and moments of deep distress. In these difficult times, it's easy to feel overwhelmed, wondering where God is in the midst of the struggle. But hardship is not a sign of His absence; rather, it is an opportunity to deepen our trust in Him and allow our character to be refined.

The Bible reminds us in **James 1:2-4 (NIV):** *"Consider it pure joy, my brothers and sisters, whenever you face trials of many kinds, because you know that the testing of your faith produces perseverance. Let perseverance finish its work so that you may be mature and complete, not lacking anything."*

Instead of allowing distress to consume us with fear and doubt, we can choose to see trials as a path to spiritual growth. Trusting God in difficult times doesn't happen overnight—it is a daily decision to rely on His promises, surrender our fears, and allow Him to strengthen our character. Here are some daily practices to help cultivate trust in God and grow through life's challenges.

Daily Suggestions for Trusting God and Growing in Character

1. Start Your Day with Prayer and Surrender

Before the worries of the day take over, begin with a moment of prayer. Surrender your fears, doubts, and challenges to God, acknowledging that He is in control.

Philippians 4:6-7 (NIV) reassures us: *"Do not be anxious about anything, but in every situation, by prayer and petition, with thanksgiving, present your requests to God. And the peace of God,* *which transcends all understanding, will guard your hearts and your minds in Christ Jesus."*

Daily Practice: Each morning, take time to pray and give God your concerns. Speak them out loud, write them in a journal, and trust that He is already working on your behalf.

2. Meditate on God's Promises

When life feels uncertain, anchor yourself in God's Word. His promises remind us that He is faithful, He sees our struggles, and He will never abandon us.

Isaiah 41:10 (NIV) encourages us: *"So do not fear, for I am with you; do not be dismayed, for I am your God. I will strengthen you and help you; I will uphold you with my righteous right hand."*

Daily Practice: Choose a Bible verse each day that speaks to trust, peace, and strength. Write it down, memorize it, or repeat it whenever fear creeps in.

3. Focus on What You Can Control and Leave the Rest to God

Worrying about things beyond our control only leads to stress and frustration. Instead, focus on what you can do—pray, take action where possible, and trust God with the outcome.

Proverbs 3:5-6 (NIV) reminds us: *"Trust in the Lord with all your heart and lean not on your own understanding; in all your ways submit to him, and he will make your paths straight."*

Daily Practice: When you feel overwhelmed, make a list of what you can control and what you need to release to God. Let go of the things that are beyond your reach.

4. Choose Gratitude Over Worry

Even in distress, there are blessings to be found. Gratitude shifts our focus from what is wrong to what is still good, reminding us of God's faithfulness.

1 Thessalonians 5:16-18 (NIV) instructs us: *"Rejoice always, pray continually, give thanks in all circumstances; for this is God's will for you in Christ Jesus."*

Daily Practice: Keep a gratitude journal. Each evening, write down three things you are thankful for, even on the hardest days.

5. Surround Yourself with Faithful Encouragement

Trusting God is easier when you are surrounded by people who uplift and encourage you. Community helps remind us that we are not alone in our struggles.

Hebrews 10:24-25 (NIV) says: *"And let us consider how we may spur one another on toward love and good deeds, not giving up meeting together, as some are in the habit of doing, but encouraging one another."*

Daily Practice: Connect with a friend, mentor, or faith-based group. Share your burdens, pray together, and seek encouragement from those who trust in God's faithfulness.

6. Reflect on How Challenges Are Strengthening Your Character

Difficult times refine us, making us stronger, wiser, and more dependent on God. Instead of asking, "Why is this happening?" ask, "How is God growing me through this?"

Romans 5:3-4 (NIV) teaches us: *"Not only so, but we also glory in our sufferings, because we know that suffering produces perseverance; perseverance, character; and character, hope."*

Daily Practice: At the end of each day, reflect on how you responded to challenges. Did you lean on God? Did you grow in patience, faith, or resilience? Recognizing growth will encourage you to keep trusting.

Final Thought:

Trusting God in times of distress isn't about ignoring difficulties—it's about knowing that He is with us through them all. Hard times are opportunities for growth, shaping our character, and drawing us closer to Him. As we practice surrender, prayer, gratitude, and reflection, we will find our trust in God deepening and our faith becoming unshakable.

Psalm 46:1 (NIV) declares: *"God is our refuge and strength, an ever-present help in trouble."*

Whatever you are facing today, remember: You are not alone. God is walking with you, strengthening your heart, and using every challenge to mold you into the person He created you to be. Keep trusting, keep growing, and let His peace fill your heart.

Walking in Faith: Finding Peace, Strength, and Purpose On Your Journey

**Walking in Faith: Finding Peace, Strength, and Purpose
On Your Journey**

AUTHOR'S NOTE

As this book comes to a close, I hope its words have inspired, uplifted, and encouraged you on your own journey of faith. Life is a winding road, full of lessons, challenges, and moments of grace, and through it all, we are never alone.

God walks with us, guiding our steps, strengthening our hearts, and surrounding us with a community of love and support. I hope you have been encouraged and inspired to draw closer to God, trust Him more deeply, and embrace the abundant life He has planned for you.

To my loyal followers—the incredible "porch and road family"—your encouragement has been a beacon of light, reminding me daily of the power of faith, friendship, and unwavering belief. Your love and support have helped shape this book, and for that, I am forever grateful.

May we all continue to seek God, walk in the footsteps of Jesus, and share His love with the world. This is not the end—only the beginning of the next chapter in our journey.

Blessings and love,
Kay

ABOUT THE AUTHOR

Kay was born in Vermont and spent over 32 years working in a small town in New Hampshire. After retiring, she embraced a life of adventure, moving to Florida before setting out to travel the country full-time. Nearly two years on the road led her to find a home in Tennessee, though her love for exploration keeps her on the move in her motorhome, always looking for the next great adventure.

Kay's spiritual journey began in 2009, but it deepened in profound ways when she started sharing devotional readings on her Facebook page. What began as daily reflections soon evolved into a deeper exploration of faith, inspiring the articles in this book. Her journey toward spiritual enlightenment continues to be a remarkable and transformative experience—one she hopes will inspire others as well.

Facebook: Messages From The Road   YouTube: Messages From The Road

www.ingramcontent.com/pod-product-compliance
Lightning Source LLC
Chambersburg PA
CBHW070851050426
42453CB00012B/2147